Gather

Gather

Cynthia Pappas

Copyright © 2021 Cynthia Pappas
All rights reserved.
Published in the United States of America
First Printing: 2021
ISBN: 978-1-935516-03-3

Cover design by Sherri Van Ravenhorst

Published by
Coincidental Communications, LLC
P.O. Box 11511
Eugene, OR 97440

Coincidental
Communications

Contents

Introduction

Place Based 1
Writing While Farming 5
Vera Vogue: Haute Couture for the Working Class. 10
Sewing Seeds of Love 13
How to Find My Elementary School. 16
The Queen of Dessert 20
Timing 25
On Reading 34
Both/And. 39
Sewing Frenzy. 44
Collecting and Recollecting 47
Reunion Reflections 50
Livestock Lessons in Leadership. 54
My Life Is Not *Mingle* Magazine. 58
Cooking Up Compassion 64
Love Letter to Malheur National Wildlife Refuge. 67
Birding the Andes. 72
Home: An Oasis and Endless To-Do List. 85
The Mundane and the Miracle 88
Celebrating Sixty in Bozeman 93
Grandparent Camp. 98
Swimming Lessons. 108
In the Vegetable Garden. 112
Out on a Limb 116
Pilates 1.0. 119
Autumnal Equinox Reset 126
A Pig Named Noelle 133
Cycles and Circles 138
Grandma's Quilts 141
Sunrise. Make Hay. Sunset 144

Acknowledgments

Introduction

Most of these essays were written prior to the 2020 coronavirus pandemic, back when life was "normal" and we could fly to visit our granddaughters on the East Coast, host dinner parties, and be in small spaces with lots of people without the worry of spreading viral droplets. Indeed, even the title of this book conjures up images of things we can no longer safely do—gather with extended family, celebrate with alumni at a college reunion, or fly to exotic destinations to bird with impunity.

Putting this collection together allowed me to focus my attention on something pleasurable and seemingly productive during this strange, suspended time. We were told not to worry about being productive; indeed, we were told to invest in our mental health, indulge in self-care (not one of my superpowers), conduct activities outdoors, keep our windows open, and limit the size of our bubble. We've become familiar with a new lexicon—viral load, socially distancing, antibody testing, masking up, zoom fatigue, vaccination trial stage efficacy, flattening the curve, and asymptomatic spread.

In "Grandparent Camp," the prohibition to screen time that I reference has all changed with the pandemic and distance learning. The older granddaughter's school curriculum is completely online, and both her piano lessons and church choir are virtual. The younger granddaughter's dance class is remote. The last essay—"Sunrise. Make Hay. Sunset."—was written four months into quarantine when we had to find a way to run our hay crew in a COVID-responsible manner.

As I write this the first vaccines for COVID-19 are rolling out across the United States, but the pandemic has touched every phase of our lives this year. I had manic mask-making days and sleepless nights filled with weird dreams. During the initial days of sheltering in place we filled our time with a strange combination of hopeful and end-of-days actions. We Marie Kondo-ized our bedroom closet. We reviewed our wills. We fertilized the hay pasture. We planted our vegetable garden. I walked every day to stay tethered to the world.

With the stories in this collection, however, I made a conscious decision to focus on warm and cozy and to indulge in my desire for comfort. As Wendell Berry says, though you have considered all the facts, choose to be joyful.

Place Based

The world is full of magical things, patiently waiting for our senses to grow sharper.
—W.B. Yeats

I planted myself on this sixty-six-acre farm in the McKenzie River watershed in Western Oregon more than thirty years ago when I married my farmer husband. The farm is all pasture grass now but used to be planted in row crops and raspberries. George has lived on the property for almost fifty years. The expanse looking north, toward the Coburg Hills, gives me breathing room. After living for twenty-six years in a city, the deep quiet was initially disorienting. As I learned the stories of the animals and plants that live here and their songs and sounds, I began to rewild my soul.

It was unintentional at first, the noticing. But then it became intentional as I started to mark arrivals and anniversaries of plants and animals on my calendar. What day did the tree swallows return in April? How many clutches of California quail hatched last year? What day did we harvest our first asparagus from the west patch? When did the osoberry bloom last year? When do the great egrets return to forage in the creek?

Even after moving to the farm I was still CEO of a regional nonprofit, and weekdays consisted of heading to work in the early morning dark and coming home from work in the dark. Initially, I didn't have focus for the fresh, astringent smell of the witch hazel blooming nor did I notice the soft pink Lenten roses braving winter's chill to fill the yard with blossoms—all tangible signs of winter's end and the start of a new season. Since retiring more than half a decade ago, I spend more time on the farm and am opening fully to the richness of this place. Merging my life with the seasons and the soil reminds me to celebrate small miracles all year long.

In early spring, a doe with her sweet twins bed down near the creek. I often see them crossing our road, heading toward the river where they forage for breakfast. Mom crosses first, handily clearing the six-foot-high pasture fence. The twins follow by scooting under the lowest strand of barbed wire.

In March the killdeer pair return to nest in the rocks between our vegetable garden and pasture. Their loud, jittering warning call keeps us guessing which slight indentation in the rocks is the actual nest. Once we find it, we focus the spotting scope on the nest and keep vigil from the living room for twenty-eight days until the young fledge.

I wake to the cheerful rise and fall of the *follow my leader* call of red-winged blackbirds, which are first to the feeders each morning. April brings the heady smell of blooming lilacs. I pick voluminous bouquets to bring spring's fragrance inside. The tightly bound buds of the dogwood awaken, spreading wide their white bracts, and tulips emerge in rainbow hues. Almost every dinner in late April includes asparagus from our patch as we try to keep up with half a pound a day. As Robin Kimmerer says in *Braiding Sweetgrass*: When we take care of the land, it takes care of us.

The miracle of deep purple clematis begins to unfurl from what appear to be dead, woody vines. Simultaneously with the currant bush blooming, Anna's hummingbirds arrive, although they don't nest on our property. It is the rufous hummingbird who will nest in the wisteria vine. At twilight we are serenaded by the incessant thrum of chorus frogs.

We wait for a couple of consecutive dry days to till the deep coffee-colored loam, then throw our energy into planting shallots, spinach, peas, broccoli, onions, potatoes, edible flowers, and cabbage. We get them into the ground in a marathon of muddy knees and bent backs, so the seeds have the benefit of the soft spring rain. We sow the remaining seeds in early May. I've learned that farmers don't do small gardens. Ours covers almost a quarter acre.

As we're getting the garden planted, tree swallows return. They swoop overhead and dart among the eight nesting boxes that we've nailed to the garden fence posts. After much squabbling, they decide who will nest where.

The landscape wears a hundred shades of green by May. When I sit on the deck and stare across the expanse of pasture to the Coburg Hills, a lightness fills my soul. The view is restful; I've learned I need this space to breathe. The pasture grass is growing and full of nutrients, so the cows no longer need to be fed hay every day. Calving season has ended. In early June the weather watch begins for that perfect seven-day window of sunny days and dry nights allowing for cutting, raking, drying, and baling hay. I walk the fields and breathe in the smell of clover. The perfume of place has seeped into my pores. When the red hot poker plant begins to bloom, black-headed grosbeaks and Bullock's orioles arrive in all their raucousness.

July, August, and September are glorious reward for slogging through the wet winter and spring. We eat dinner on the back deck and linger with a glass of wine until it's too dark at 10 pm to clear the dishes. Every meal is harvested from the garden, thirty feet from our back door.

We measure our wealth by growing enough to give away.

There is always work to do on the farm. But I like to work. Engaging in an intimacy with the land keeps me grounded so I don't live in my head. Intellectualizing is nowhere near as fulfilling as getting my hands dirty and calloused. Tending the land and making meals from plants grown in the garden create a filament that runs from my hands to my heart.

The gifts of this place are many. The hooded merganser pair, on the best-dressed duck list, paddle in the creek. We pick blackberries along the edge of our pasture in August with our granddaughters and make ice cream. At day's end I sit in the hot tub to soak my tired muscles. The great horned owl has returned and is looking for a mate. From his perch in the cedar tree, he glides silently over the tub, frequenting our pasture on his hunting forays. So much beauty and breathing space. I stretch my skin in the summer months to capture as much vitamin D as possible before the winter months of cozying-in begin.

I feel rich in the number of bird species that frequent our place. I wasn't a birder before I moved to the farm. I thrill to the laughing *wuck wuck* of the pileated woodpecker couple who feed in the cottonwood snag along Cedar Creek. Osprey chirp high overhead, floating on updrafts in the cobalt sky. The shy, solitary white-breasted nuthatch feeds at our sunflower feeder under cover of the maple. I watch him most mornings out the kitchen window. A stocky belted kingfisher perches low over the creek, emitting a constant *chiddering* rattle.

This farm has imprinted itself deeply into my DNA; I can no longer imagine living anywhere else. I am home. This is where my story is written.

Writing While Farming

I'm "retired." However, living on a sixty-six-acre farm is not very retiring. We raise grass-fed beef. Ours is only a small herd, but the work still involves calving in the spring, castrating calves in the summer, feeding hay in the fall and winter, and keeping the pasture green in the summer by moving irrigation pipe every day.

My avocation is writing; it's a pleasure, a compulsion, my way of communicating with the world. I'm not recommending that you adopt my writing process because it is a bit erratic, nor am I touting it as some sterling method for producing major literary work. Some use the ritual of lighting a candle to get in the proper space to write. Instead, I'm burning the candle at both ends.

I try to handwrite or key in raw story ideas while they are swimming in my head. A staccato burst of words, usually based on an image I've been ruminating about. Get those first ill-formed thoughts on paper, then try to link several images into a coherent skeleton of an idea. I might have an hour if I'm lucky. It's deep July and the irrigation pipe needs to be moved. While moving pipe I think about using similes and metaphors so my writing doesn't sound shallow and dull. I try to remember to avoid clichés, because I do have a cliché affliction.

After moving pipe each morning, it's time to harvest what has ripened overnight in our vegetable garden. That usually includes tomatoes, cucumbers, beans, poblano peppers, yellow squash, zucchini, snow peas, and jalapenos. When I open the garden gate there is a furious flapping of stubby wings as quail fly out helter-skelter from under protective rows of corn. The lead quail *tsktsktsks* rapidly in alarm without taking a breath. I worry that I may be inducing tiny quail heart attacks. While I'm picking, my mind wanders. I'm trying to recall whether the story I'm writing references all five senses. It's so much easier to recognize this when I am outside engaging all my senses.

I munch on snow peas and beans; they snap satisfyingly as I bite into them. The fresh smell of tomato vines intoxicates as I pluck the red orbs. Kneeling in the dust on my hands and knees to hunt for cucumbers hiding underneath prickly leaves, I hesitate slightly before reaching in to give garter snakes a chance to squiggle away. An hour later, after I've watered the garden and sorted the produce and put it in bags, I sit down at my computer for about twenty minutes to note ideas that need fleshing out in the story I'm composting, er, I mean composing. These snippets are always typed in bold and in parentheses so I can easily locate and quickly return to them (next time I have twenty minutes).

My husband arrives home from an outing with a gift of fifty pounds of Asian pears he picked at our friend's orchard. The pears need to be sorted, peeled, sliced, and put in the food dryer before they rot. As I place the sliced pears on the drying racks, new sentences take shape. I love the idea of spending the winter eating fruit that tastes of sweet summer.

When I have a short break from farm work, I read what I've written so far. Have I started my story with action that will pull the reader in? I realize I haven't. But then I get distracted. We are without clean work clothes. These same clothes also serve as walking-around-town clothes, and we can't smell like manure tonight at book group.

I separate the jeans and t-shirts that have cow poop on them from the delicates and throw a load in the laundry.

Okay, back to my review. Have I used alliteration? Hyperbole? Onomatopoeia? An allusion? Personification? Have I merely described a situation and not made it into a story? This list of questions is not a formula, per se, but more of a reminder to myself. It is much more clear in farming when the job is finished. With writing, it's difficult to know when to cut the cord. Yikes, there I go with my cliché affliction.

It is my turn to host book group, which means the lawn has to be mowed—an hour and a half on a riding lawnmower. I've timed it. Nothing small or quick happens on this farm. We'll discuss our book out on the deck because I haven't had time to clean the house. I hose the dust from the deck and set the table for dinner. Because my book group believes it's good to break bread together, a full dinner is expected, plus the host is required to do research about the author and lead the discussion. Gaack! I would be happy with a book group that just meets for wine and dessert and, of course, an opportunity to discuss the book.

This week I also happen to be hosting members of my writing critique group, who believe dessert is sufficient. Oatmeal cookies will do. I accidently burn the raisins while they're on the stove "plumping" in their own juices, because I'm also trying to talk to my sister on the phone (a conversation way overdue) and pay bills. I have to start over. I'm enamored with the idea of multi-tasking, but sometimes it just doesn't work out. When I add the new, non-burned raisin juice to the bowl, the batter becomes slick and wet. So I add some more oatmeal. When the cookies come out of the oven, they look dry. Never mess with a baking recipe, says my husband, who has changed up every recipe I've ever seen him make.

Okay. Back to writing. I have sent out a draft of a story to my writing critique group for their review. It's due to the local newspaper in five days, and I can't find an ending. The ending is flabby. It's not pertinent to the story. It doesn't sing. I give it to George to read and say, "Help. Where is the thread? What is the purpose of this article?" And, just like that, his advice allows me to tie a bow on it and be done.

On Saturday we decline an invitation to go wine tasting with friends because we must button up the farm for fall. These friends wonder why we don't have more free time; after all, we are both RETIRED. We have almost 250 pounds of paste tomatoes (I am not exaggerating) that we need to DO SOMETHING with. We rev into high gear and boil, peel, cut, and can twenty-eight quarts of diced tomatoes. We boil down thirty pounds of tomatoes, drop in a cheesecloth spice ball, leave the pot to simmer, and end up with six pints of catsup. We quarter fifty pounds of tomatoes; dust them with salt, pepper, and dried basil; and put them in the food dehydrator, charmingly called Harvest Maid. I try not to hold this against the men who most likely thought this was a clever and appropriate name. All this standing in the kitchen doing rote work provides ample time to think about different ways to phrase certain sentences. If I come up with a winner I try to remember it until I can run upstairs to my computer and insert the new phraseology.

I am composing another piece about how I have more time to be present in the moment since retirement, which leads to deeper observations about the wildlife that inhabits our farm. I feel like a bit of a hypocrite actually writing the story because, if truth be told, it can only be completed in half-hour bursts of writing before I'm interrupted to help my husband load the truck for a trip to the dump. But during those half hours, I'm completely present in the moment. Our trashcans and recyclables are overflowing, so it has become the next emergent issue. After that, it's almost three hours of mowing the pasture for thistle control. These hours driving our John Deere tractor with a pull-behind bat-wing mower in large mindless circles allow me to ruminate on how to finish the present-in-the-moment story. Endings do tend to elude me.

There are two things in the comics section today that I want to incorporate into a story. "I didn't lie! I just botoxed the truth." "The purr doesn't lie." Who knew the funny pages could be such an important source of literary inspiration? I scribble them on a note and stick it to my computer screen.

Then something inevitably breaks. Today it's the food dehydrator. It's loaded to the brim with slices of Asian pears when my husband plugs it in and nothing happens. Maybe the Harvest Maid has decided to rise up in protest over her place in life, silent and in the kitchen. I hover around, providing what I feel is much-needed moral support while George curses and bangs on things. Amazingly, he's quite successful in getting things to work again. My role of hand-wringing plays no small part in this success.

Back at the computer for an hour of finish work. I hit send on three stories where I've matched an appropriate magazine to the essay topic and feel a shiver of anticipation that someone, somewhere, might say yes.

Vera Vogue: Haute Couture for the Working Class

The *whirrr* of the sewing machine was the soundtrack of my childhood; Mom was always sewing. She was a controlled rumble of a woman, a complicated Vogue pattern. Besides working a part-time job in an elementary school cafeteria, keeping the household, cooking all our meals, leading the PTA, serving as co-leader of my Girl Scout troop, being a wife, sewing Barbie's entire wardrobe, and raising two girls, Mom found time to make all of our clothes.

I thought Mom was born knowing how to sew. Her patience and skill amazed me. Her mom must have passed that talent on to Mom through her genes. When I was growing up, Grandma lived with us and was always making quilts: Double Nine-Patch, Star of Bethlehem, Double Wedding Ring, Flower Garden. She sewed them all by hand, twelve stitches to the inch.

Mom must have passed the talent on to me. I started sewing early, and by 1974 when I was in tenth grade, I'd mastered McCalls and Butterick patterns. They were straightforward and had limited numbers of pattern pieces. Vogue patterns, the crème de la crème, remained off-limits. At four dollars, they were too expensive for the family budget, too complicated, and usually required yards and yards of fabric.

In my family, "vogue" conveyed the height of elegance and fashion. But we called Mom's creations *Vera*

Vogue, coining the phrase with my mother's middle name, pleased with the alliteration. One wouldn't want to be caught wearing the opposite of Vera Vogue—Mode O' Day. For my mom, that dress shop moniker conveyed frumpiness. Mode O' Day started selling dresses in 1932 during the depths of the Depression. Those dresses were manufactured by the dozens, so you never wore an original. Perhaps the styles were too tame for my mom's taste. She poo-pooed them.

When sister Sallie got invited to the senior prom, Mom decided that the occasion warranted splurging. Sallie got to pick a Vogue pattern for her dress. She chose Vogue Americana (1043), designed by Oscar de la Renta. We bought the pattern on a trip to Baron's Fabrics in the San Fernando Valley on April 10, 1974. Forty-six years later I still have the date-stamped pattern in my pattern box.

With 13 pattern pieces—and an underlining for the bodice, midriff, and front and back neckline—it was as complex a pattern as I'd ever seen my mom sew. The gathered skirt was finished with a wide hemline ruffle. Sallie chose white lace with a lining of turquoise taffeta the color of glacial run-off. That icy blue-and-white fabric combination evoked swirling whitewater.

Because the dress was lined, Mom basically had two dresses to finish that month—the outer lace confection and the underlying taffeta. The pattern required almost seven yards of lace and four yards of taffeta. When Sallie put on the dress, she looked like a prescient version of Princess Elsa of *Frozen*. The dress transformed her into a frothy exaltation of icy turquoise sophistication. I coveted that dress the way a foodie lusts after dinner at the French Laundry.

I couldn't wait for Sallie to leave for college so I could see what it felt like to wear that dress. A year later when I was in eleventh grade, a young man named Andy invited me to the prom. Even though I never gave him any encouragement, I knew he was smitten from the love notes he would slip into my locker. I thought of him as nothing more than a nice guy, but his invitation was a vehicle to *wear the dress.*

For me, clothes have never been about the designer. It's always been about how the clothes make me feel. When I looked at a pattern, could I envision myself as bold? Quirky? Elegant? Hip? Making my own clothes has allowed me to try on many personalities over the years. The style I keep coming back to is one of integration—my physical appearance unified with how I feel inside.

That hand-me-down prom dress was what I had coveted. I wore the dress to fulfill my princess fantasy, but I didn't feel like a princess inside. It felt wrong to wear the dress when my heart wasn't really in it. Only when my head and heart are aligned does fashion become more than a statement, it becomes a style.

Sewing Seeds of Love

When spring flowers start blooming, I always think of my mother. My mind wanders back to her lovingly tended flower garden and the Easter dresses she patiently created that echoed those beautiful blossoms.

I have my own garden now. But I still miss the annual rite of spring—a new dress for Easter. I page through family photo albums that I've pulled from the bookshelf. Tina Campt, the author of *Listening to Images,* theorizes that photographs are haptic artifacts, capable of transmitting frequencies that can be felt or heard by the body.

The photos of my sister Sallie and me, dating back to 1961, place me immediately in my childhood home. The house is in a subdivision of other ranch-style houses with huge backyards. We are standing in the hot sun in our new Easter dresses. I am three and Sallie is five. Our dresses are paper white like the birch saplings in the yard. The square collars are trimmed in white lace. Sallie wears a pink bow in her hair.

In 1962, Sallie and I pose in our new dresses on the expanse of grass in a backyard that has not yet experienced the full ministrations of my mother's loving touch. There is only a small bed planted in ranunculus. Each dress, like a ranunculus, has a translucent voile "apron" over voluminous amounts of ethereal pink cotton fabric gathered at the waist. Pigtails with pink ribbons sprout from behind my ears. As I look at my pig-tailed image from long ago, I can feel the stretch of my forehead as my hair is pulled tightly into those two rubber bands.

In the photo from 1963, we wear matching periwinkle dresses the color of bearded iris with smocked bodices and full, gathered waists. The exuberant ruffling at the neck and sleeve echoes undulating iris petals, now glorious in the garden. It was the first time Mom attempted smocking and she said "never again." I agreed. I had to try that dress on too many times until she got the "fit" just right. Getting the dress off while keeping the puffed sleeves pinned in place was tricky.

By 1964, apricot, peach, and plum trees flourish in the backyard. A bird bath is filled with water. Iris, agapanthus, and calla lilies spill from the beds lining the lawn. Our white dresses with rounded collars and celery green satin sashes match the unfurling calla lily petal and stamen.

In the 1965 photo, both Sallie and I wear rayon polkadot dresses with an inverted pleat running vertically from the empire waist, adorned with a white bow. Lavender agapanthus reimagined into a dress. The photo evokes a taste memory of our ham and scalloped potato Easter meal.

In 1966, I would have been eight. Our sleeveless dresses are bright yellow, like jonquils. Wide, white grosgrain ribbon encircles the dropped waist separating the bodice from the pleated skirt. White wrist-length gloves and white patent leather Mary Janes complete our outfits. Our daffodil-yellow socks perfectly match the dress fabric, and the air smells like lily of the valley. I look so gangly that year, all coltish legs. In a separate photo, Mom is wearing an exuberant orange dress that echoes the riotous trumpet vine cascading from the bedroom window trellis. Her orange lipstick matches perfectly.

March 19, 1967. We are at Mission San Juan Capistrano sitting by the fountain to witness the annual return of the cliff swallows. Mom had to finish our dresses early that year so we could wear them to see the swallows complete their six-thousand-mile migration from Argentina. Sallie's dress, white with an olive green print, has a double ribbon of velvet at the waist. Mine is a black-and-white print adorned with black velvet ribbon. The colors mirror the deep green and dark shadows of the fountain pool.

Mom's beautiful, home-sewn Easter dresses appeared religiously, year after year. It occurs to me now that they were a perfect metaphor for my childhood. Presented to the world, polished and shining, a manifestation of Mom's love. Oregon author Brian Doyle described this as "a way to say something for which we don't have particularly good words."

Mom's love language was sewing and gardening. Her tender care and loving touch resulted in her girls and her garden blossoming in the parched California desert. I feel Mom's presence when I'm in my garden and at the sewing machine, planting beauty, sharing gifts from my hand and heart.

How to Find My Elementary School

Meet me at the home where I grew up for the first sixteen years of my life. My house is three down from the corner on Runnymede Street in Canoga Park, California.

When we first moved in, all the land across the wash from our house was planted in orange groves that went on as far as I could walk. The smell of those blossoms was intoxicating. In the 1950s when Los Angeles County was the most prosperous agricultural county in America, there were forty-one thousand acres of orange groves. Acre by acre they disappeared, and subdivisions sprung up in their place.

In 1964 I'm in the first grade and I already know the way to school. When I was in kindergarten, I rode to school on my mom's faded purple Schwinn three-speed, astride a gold pillow from our couch balanced on top of the bike rack behind her seat. She pedaled the bike as I held on to her waist. Kindergarten met for only a half-day, so I got home before my sister. In Mrs. Wainwright's class we learned about dinosaurs. One day we drew a chalk outline of a brontosaurus on the asphalt playground. It was so big, all thirty-two children in my class could stand inside it and there was still room for another kindergarten class to join us in its belly. I love everything about kindergarten—my teacher, my classmates, learning. Learning the best of all.

How to Find My Elementary School

In first grade I am eager every morning to leave for school with my sister, who's in third grade. From our yellow house with the white trim we'll walk a long block, past thirteen other ranch-style stucco houses until we turn left onto Royer Avenue. Along the way, my friend David will be waiting for us in front of his house. Sometimes we run into Roberta when we turn onto Royer Avenue. Every house on our block has kids my age. The Reigears and Armstrongs bookend our house, and the Spauldings live across the street. The Degnars' house is on the corner, and the Mayer boys live next to them. Further down the street are the Bauders and the Carters. We all play together.

My metal lunchbox has a picture of Barbie on the front. She bangs against my leg when I swing my arms. Inside is a peanut-butter-and-grape-jelly sandwich on white Wonder bread, an apple, milk in a tiny thermos, and two homemade chocolate chip cookies. My sister has a Green Hornet lunchbox. On our walk we pass crepe myrtle trees. We set our lunchboxes down and pop the tight buds open to reveal ruffled fuschia-colored blossoms. The burst of pink is extremely satisfying, it hurries us toward summer.

Just two houses after we turn left, Royer Avenue dead-ends into a huge concrete wash with a trickle of greenish-blackish slime running along its length. The sides of the deep wash slant at a forty-five-degree angle. It's filled with metal shopping carts, balls that have escaped over backyard fences, trash, and tree trimmings.

Mom tells us not to go into the wash. It is full of filthy things and it stinks. But it is too enticing. We might discover some treasure, something valuable that someone lost. So we side-step down the concrete slope in our saddle shoes, careful not to get them dirty. We walk all the way back to my house and peer up into all my friends' backyards. We find Stuart's ball that got kicked over the fence, but we have to leave it there until we walk home after school. We can't stay long or we'll be late for school and then, for sure, we'll be in trouble.

We climb back out and cross the bridge spanning the wash. One side is chain link fencing but the other side is magical. The wooden fence is covered in honeysuckle vine. It smells ambrosial, a fragrance that even now I never tire of inhaling. We stop to do some honeysuckling—by pulling the delicate stamens from their blossoms, a drop of nectar is revealed at the base. We suck the nectar into our mouths, imagining we could survive on this and nothing else.

Once across the bridge, a dirt path runs along the edge of a field of corn and strawberries. Mary, we call her "The Strawberry Lady," has a fruit stand where she sells her produce from the field. At the very end of the school year there are red, ripe strawberries and corn starting to tassel. The symmetrical rows in the field create a sense of order. It's hot, even early in the morning, and the Santa Ana winds carry the dry smell of soil.

At the end of the field is West Hills Hospital, a one-story concrete bunker-like building.

We follow the path all the way to the intersection with Sherman Way, where the grandmotherly crossing guard holds her red STOP sign. She wears a tan cap, khaki pedal pushers, and pink lipstick. She waits until enough kids have gathered. Then she looks both ways and marches ahead of us right out into the middle of the street. She is so brave.

After we cross, it's only another quick block then a left turn onto Enadia Way. The tall, black metal gates of Enadia Way Elementary School rise near the corner parking lot. The trip takes about twenty minutes from my house.

I attend the same elementary school all the way through sixth grade. School is never boring for me. When I'm finished with school for the day, I play school at home with my friend from across the street. I am always the teacher. I mimic my beloved teachers. I love school. The smell of chalk. The workbooks with penciled answers on each page. Learning cursive. The kind teachers who call on me when I raise my hand. Learning to read and construct sentences. My parents tell me an education is something you will always have; no one can take it away from you. I take this to heart.

The Queen of Dessert

George requested a Charlotte Rousse cake to celebrate his birthday. I never heard of such a thing and that says a lot having been raised by the Queen of Dessert. I Googled it. You could make it either the easy way or the hard way—buy store-bought ladyfingers or pipe your own. I chose to pipe my own because homemade always tastes better. I outlined a pattern on parchment paper and squeezed out sponge cake into twenty-four ladyfingers of equal mass and length. They would line the inside of a six-inch-deep straight-sided glass pan. To form the base of the cake, I piped sponge cake onto the parchment paper in the form of a nautilus.

As I'm piping, I'm transported to my childhood kitchen, watching my mother's hands wield the piping bag to decorate a cake. They are large-veined hands with pronounced knuckles. Working hands. Hands that were rarely still.

The sponge cake didn't disappoint. Each ladyfinger was light and airy and stood up around the inside of the pan like riders on the Tilt-a-Whirl at the carnival. I beat together whipped cream and diced strawberries for the filling and topped the concoction with huge ripe strawberries, tips pointed to the sky. Mom would have been proud.

When I was in fourth grade, Mom took an eight-week cake decorating class with her best friend, Jackie. It was at the Shadow Ranch Park recreation room and met weekly. After registering for the class, she had to buy a set of Wilton's metal cake tips. Twenty-four tips with different shapes in a special plastic case. She purchased funnel-shaped plastic-coated fabric pouches to hold the icing. When they were filled, she screwed a metal cake tip onto the pointed end of the fabric. The icing squeezed from the funnel in the shape of the tip. Magic.

After school when Mom arrived home from her part-time job, my sister and I watched her do her homework. First she'd bake a sheet cake, then carefully remove it from the pan after it had cooled. She did this by pressing a cooling rack against the golden top of the cake and turning the whole thing upside down, releasing the cake from the pan. Then she repeated this process, only this time a piece of plywood covered in aluminum foil was placed against the bottom of the cake so it would land right side up on its presentation surface. She made a pattern out of parchment paper. When the cake cooled, she placed the pattern on top of the cake and sliced up and down with a sharp knife, following the outline, to cut out the pieces of cake that were not integral to the design.

That's where the best part came in. After licking the beaters, we scavenged the superfluous cake scraps. And we were allowed to use a little bit of the icing that was so sweet it made my gums hurt.

Mom would divide the frosting into separate bowls and dye it with food coloring. For a wedding shower cake, one bowl of frosting was dyed red for the upside down scalloping around the edge of the umbrella and the piping that defined the ribs of the umbrella.

For some of the cakes, it wasn't just a process of subtracting the cake that wouldn't be used in the design. It was a geometry problem involving gluing pieces of sheet cake together with icing to construct a new shape. For the baby shower cake, she cut the cake into the shape of a baby's jacket. She dyed the icing light blue and applied it to resemble a crochet stitch. She used a thin ribbon of icing to form a bow at the neckline.

One week, Mom made a cake that was a doll's ruffled skirt by draping wide icing layers around the center of an angel food cake. At the point where each swath draped, there was an icing rose to secure it. Barbie stood in the middle of the cake; her icing skirt was purple, my favorite color. Mom was a master at making dreams like this happen.

The following week, the class assignment was a sheet cake adorned with a design each student created. Mom chose to do a backyard scene with a built-in swimming pool, a flagstone path, and green grass. The flagstones were made of gray Necco wafers. The water in the pool was a turquoise translucent gel and the grass was kelly-green icing.

The fourth week, each member of the class created a bikini cake. Hostess Snowballs were used to form the bra of the suit and the waist was carved out on each side. The bikini bottom was all icing. I don't recall the color of the swimsuit, just that the large bosom was embarrassing to a flat-chested ten-year-old.

One of the round cake assignments was a square-dancing troupe with hands joined around the outer edge of the cake. Each square dancer was made of a Tootsie Roll lollipop head and icing body.

Why I remain so fascinated with these sweet cake memories 50 years later is something I'm still trying to understand. Maybe these cakes were Mom's way of being heard. Mom didn't get a career. She got my sister and me and supported Dad in his engineering career. Although she had a part-time job in an elementary school cafeteria, it didn't define her like Dad's job defined him.

Even now I'd much rather bake than cook. When baking I have a finished product, sometimes even a work of art, that I can admire until it is eaten. With cooking, the creation is whisked from stovetop to hungry mouths while still hot; the pleasure is in the taste, not the looks.

The best part about baking is focusing on creating one thing. It's fairly formulaic. With cooking, you're usually trying to produce three courses and have them all ready to eat at the same time. A typical dinner when I was growing up was a roast, green beans, and mashed potatoes. Mom just cooked them all the same length of time. Our vegetable side dishes always lacked any nutritional value because they had been cooked to death. And, of course, good cooks are supposed to improvise, not follow the recipe by rote. But Mom was not the kind of cook who would just "toss in what it needs" after giving it a taste. She measured everything. I understood why Mom disliked cooking. There are other more important things to do. Like make dessert. She was indefatigable in this pursuit.

The ratio of baking recipes to cooking recipes in my mother's old black-and-white metal recipe box is astounding. Half of the eleven-by-six-inch metal rectangular box is given over to recipes for cakes, pies, cookies, candies, pastry, pudding, and frosting. It sits in my kitchen where I occasionally consult it. What do these recipes say about how we ate while I was growing up? Clearly, sugar was not vilified in the Pappas kitchen. There was no ill that a goody could not salve.

One glance at the recipes, handwritten in Palmer Method cursive, and I am right back in my childhood kitchen. It's a sunny summer afternoon and Mom is mixing oatmeal, brown sugar, and dates to make my favorite date bars. The Medjools are bubbling on the stove to soften and plump. Heat emanates from the tiny cooking space. The fan is on to dissipate the sweat beading along Mom's hairline. I anticipate the gooey sweetness, but they have to cool first.

Another favorite was eating home-canned Santa Rosa plums in the middle of winter. We rescued the summer-ripe plums by diving into the deep end of the built-in swimming pool in our backyard. The plum tree branches cantilevered over the pool, creating a fun game of plum diving before they had a chance to stain the white gunite. Every time I visit California in July, I fill my belly full of Santa Rosa plums.

I've finally realized Mom's example was always about paying attention to the details. Whether it was decorating cakes, sewing clothes, finding pennies in a parking lot, gardening, or rock hounding, she collected beautiful objects and surrounded herself with things that made her happy. She was an amazingly creative woman who needed multiple outlets to satisfy that constant urge to bring something new and beautiful into the world. Everything I do—quilting, reading, creating stories, picking up pennies that I find, collecting rocks—is all a prayer to Mom.

Timing

When I was nine and my dad, Sharold, was forty-nine, he bought a blue V-8 Mustang. Through my high school years—when he figured I was old enough to learn to maintain a car—we worked together in the garage on that beloved car. I designated myself the daughter who would substitute for the son. I don't recall him ever saying I love you. He loved through action. I wanted to be in his company and be a part of that.

My father believed my sister and I could do anything. He taught me how to set the timing on our Mustang and how to change a tire. How to change the car's sparkplugs and oil. How to understand my calculus homework. The intricacies of football. To root for the Unsers of Indy 500 fame. He made sure I knew how to swim, because he didn't. He made sure I received a postgraduate education because he didn't. He was generous to a fault. And so proud. First generation immigrant proud.

According to the Ford Mustang Manual: *Without a correct timing setting you will never see a smooth or stable idle. Timing is everything. When setting the timing in your 1966 Ford Mustang it's important to know there are three types of timing: initial, centrifugal, and vacuum.*

Dad spent the weekends tinkering at his workbench in the garage, a cigarette always smoldering nearby in a clear glass ashtray. He'd solder tiny transistors and diodes onto circuit boards. Then he did something with an oscilloscope to test them. It had a green screen and showed the voltage as wave signals.

Dad was an early adopter—we had one of the first color TVs on the block. He invited neighbors and co-workers over to watch the World Series. Dad enjoyed hosting gatherings at our house, although he was not a baseball fan. He sat in the kitchen smoking, more an observer than a participant. His profound hearing loss meant he missed half of any conversation. Mom was busy in the kitchen laying out food on the table.

His co-workers called him Shay. One said, "Hey Shay, when do we get to meet those daughters you're always talking about?" Dad called us in from the backyard and proudly introduced us. One co-worker said his name was Ducey Fernandez. My sister and I heard this as Juicy Bananas, which we thought was hysterical. When we got to giggling, Dad would get a crooked little almost-smile and say, "It's going to snow." I had no idea what this meant but it made us giggle even more.

He had a soft, round face that reminded me of Desi Arnaz on TV. His hair was always neatly trimmed and gelled, like Desi's.

Sometimes the color picture on the TV would get all wavy and he'd bring in his degausser, plug it in, and crouch in front of the screen, wielding the coil, like a magician, in ever-widening loops to eliminate the magnetic field and restore the color on the screen.

Dad loved to fish. All of our family vacations were focused around camping and fishing—Mammoth Lakes, Lake Cachuma, Lake Nacimiento, the Sierras. He didn't own a boat. He was not a fly fisherman. He was a bait fisherman, casting his line from the shore. I still have stored up in the attic his blue metal tackle box full of leaders, lures, and plugs. My sister and I played Barbie along the shoreline while he fished. Mom hunted for rocks or read her murder mystery in a chair in the shade.

Daddy worked at Litton Industries in Woodland Hills in Guidance and Control on inertial navigation systems for F-15 and F-16 jets used in the Vietnam War. By the early 1960s, nearly seventy percent of the San Fernando Valley's one million residents were dependent on the defense and aerospace industries. Litton—along with Rocketdyne, Bunker-Ramo, Teledyne, Lockheed, Northrop, Douglas, and Rockwell aviation companies—were all major employers. He worked so much overtime for production of those two planes during those war years that we hardly saw him at home except at dinner and on weekends. But somehow in the midst of family and work, he made time to attend night school at the local community college to earn a degree in electrical engineering. His work ethic was gargantuan. He got that from his father, who ran a restaurant.

All classic Mustangs are equipped with four-cycle gasoline engines. The four cycles are intake, compression, power, and exhaust. An engine produces power from these four cycles by mixing air and fuel into a vapor before entering the combustion chamber above the piston.

When gasoline vaporizes in an engine cylinder it can ignite with explosive force, which makes heat and pressure that moves the engine's pistons, the crankshaft, transmission, and ultimately the drive wheels.

I can picture Dad in his brown wingtips mowing the lawn. Were those the only shoes he owned? He was never one to dress down. Always wore pressed chinos and a button-down shirt, even on the weekends when the shirt was short-sleeved. He smelled of Mennen Skin Bracer Aftershave. I still have the bottle that he was using before he died, thirty-six years ago. All I have to do is unscrew the cap on that bottle of emerald green liquid and I am rocketed back in time to my parents' bathroom watching my dad shave as he got ready for work each morning. I would sit on the closed lid of the toilet, staring up at him, fascinated that he never cut himself with the blade of that razor. He was a slight man with a Greek uni-brow of thick, black hair. His brow and forehead were raised in perpetual surprise. I wonder if that's because he couldn't hear what was going on most of the time. He was completely deaf in one ear and partially deaf in the other, from a childhood case of mumps. He wore a pair of horn-rimmed bifocals with hearing aids attached at the end of each earpiece.

One of the loves in my dad's life was our beagle, Maverick. When Dad was home, Maverick followed him around looking for treats and affection. When Dad watched TV from his corner chair, Maverick always sat at his feet, the object of loving attention. I sometimes wished I was Maverick.

In 1970 when I was entering junior high, my parents splurged on a built-in swimming pool in our backyard. I remember that pool was paid for, month by month, through pay coupons. The stack never seemed to diminish. With much anticipation, we watched the pool construction crew dig a nine-foot-deep hole in our lawn that shallowed out to three feet at one end. A major decision was: diving board or slide. "Slide!" Sallie and I chorused in unison. We had pool parties every summer through junior high and high school. The Fourth of July party was the highlight. Everyone brought potluck and Mom always carved a watermelon into a basket shape with serrated edges and filled it with melon balls, grapes, strawberries, and diced apples. The kids played Marco Polo and practiced their cannon balls. The adults smoked and argued politics.

Dad was a stern teacher. When one of us girls disappointed him by not living up to his expectations, you received the Silent Treatment. This was more painful than any kind of physical punishment. More dismissive than a voice raised in anger. It was the absence of his presence. It didn't happen often, because you did your best to never disappoint. After his generosity, his indulgences, his time and attention, you could rarely justify doing something that would disappoint him. I recall once slamming my bedroom door on him when he wouldn't let me go somewhere with my friends, even though I had washed the dishes and finished my homework. I had already been out three evenings that week to meet up with girlfriends and he decided a fourth evening out wasn't warranted. His argument didn't make sense to my seventeen-year-old self. Only later did I realize he wanted to spend time with me. Why couldn't he have simply just expressed that? It was exasperating, but I did not yet have the ability to understand why. I'm not sure I do even now.

Timing refers to adjusting the moment of firing of the spark plug during the compression stroke. When the piston begins its journey back to the top of the cylinder bore, it compresses the fuel and air against the top of the cylinder. As the piston nears the top of the cylinder bore, the spark plug fires, igniting the fuel/air mixture.

Heat and pressure created during ignition exert force on the piston, pushing it downward in the cylinder bore, applying pressure on the connecting rod and crankshaft. This is the power stroke. As the piston nears the bottom in the power stroke, the exhaust valve opens. The piston begins its journey back to the top of the bore, forcing exhaust gases out through the open exhaust valve. This is called the exhaust stroke.

The engines for almost every American rocket came to life amid the sandstone and sage in the mountains near my childhood home. In the Santa Susana Mountains that rose above the San Fernando Valley, loud rumbling noises often erupted from the Santa Susana Field Laboratory when they tested the big engines they were preparing to use in the Apollo space mission. Every so often on a quiet evening in the 1960s, you could hear the roar of a rocket engine and see the sky light up in the hills to the west. Sometimes sonic booms echoed from jet test flights over Edwards Air Force Base in Palmdale.

On weekend afternoons after his nap on the couch, Daddy would put on Herb Alpert and the Tijuana Brass and he and I would dance to "The Taste of Honey," me in stocking feet balanced on the top of his shoes, holding on to his hands while he danced a wild jig around the living room, the change in his pockets jingling. On those evenings, he and my mom sat out in the backyard at the picnic table, he with his Coors, she with her Screwdriver. He taught me how to search the sky for satellites.

Typically, timing is set with a timing light. A timing light is simply a strobe light which is triggered by a spark discharge on the number 1 plug. The flash produced by the timing light will illuminate marks on a crankshaft pulley. Since the timing light will "strobe" just at the instant the timing marks are in line with a pointer affixed to the engine block, the actual point of firing can be measured.

We had one car, the Mustang. Mom dropped Dad off at work so she could use the car for the day. At quitting time, my mom, sister, and I rode fifteen minutes to Litton to bring him home. He had top secret clearance so we couldn't go inside. Instead, my sister and I would wait out on the sidewalk that ran from his building to the parking lot. I was so little all I can remember is focusing on the pants of all the men who were exiting. When I recognized the cuffs and sharp creases on a pair of olive green chinos out of the hundreds streaming by, I shouted, "Daddy!" He was a man of few words, not one to show much emotion. He smiled that almost-smile and said, "Let's go, your mom's waiting."

It is critical to properly prepare your Mustang's carburetor before attempting to set an optimum idle. A rough idle can be caused by a poorly performing carburetor. Any carburetor work should be completed before timing is set. First things first.

Sometimes on the weekends, we'd drive out toward Filmore and stop for date milkshakes. Our weekend entertainment would often be to drive to Lake Lindero, or any number of new subdivisions blooming in the Conejo Valley, and walk through model homes. Were my parents ever planning to buy one and move or was it just real estate lust? Sometimes Daddy would drive us to El Segundo to watch the 707 and 727 jets take off at the end of the Los Angeles Airport runway. We'd sit on the hood of the car and fantasize about their destinations.

While Sallie was in school, Mom and I went grocery shopping. We'd visit the drive-through at the Giacopuzzi Dairy to pick up milk, then stop at the Alpha Beta grocery store. I vividly remember every week we'd come home from Alpha Beta with a carton of cigarettes—Winstons. I got the privilege of opening the carton and inserting each red-cellophane-wrapped pack into a ceramic stacker that hung on the side of the kitchen cupboard. To accomplish this I had to pull a chair over to reach the ceramic holder. Making sure Daddy had enough cigarettes to get through the week. Late evenings he sat by the kitchen window and smoked his Winstons, ash cascading off the glowing tip.

Every Friday night, Mom got a reprieve from cooking. Daddy took us to Sizzler's Steak House and splurged on T-bone steaks and fries for the family. The highlight was their bleu cheese dressing. We ate it on our salads, our fries, and our steaks. To this day the taste of that bleu cheese is my yardstick for treating myself. It is the comfort taste of my childhood. Daddy, the quiet, constant comfort in my childhood.

On Saturdays, Dad gave Sallie and me money to walk to the 7-11 with our neighbors Stuart, Cheryl, and Sue to buy Slurpees and candy bars.

One of his favorite lines was "Why go to a game when the best seats in the house are in the house." He was the ultimate homebody. The story I've always told myself is he was not a risk taker. But maybe this is not the reality. Maybe in his younger years he'd already taken all the risks he wanted. During wartime, they moved away from his family in Colorado Springs to Venice, California, betting on the fact that he and Mom could get jobs working in the shipyards.

One weekend, a girl in my senior high school class invited me and my best girlfriends to the lake to celebrate graduation. We waterskied behind a ski boat named Tacos and Bagels in honor of her Mexican mom and Jewish dad. We had such a great time.

Not long after returning home, inexplicably, my friend's father died of a heart attack. My dad was in the kitchen when I got the phone call. I started sobbing. In an uncharacteristic gesture, Daddy drew me onto his lap and I sat there wailing, burrowing into his chest. Trying to sort through my tangled thoughts of having just seen my friend's father very much alive, I think the unthinkable: What if it had been my daddy?

I recall visiting my parents one weekend after I'd moved away to attend college. Dad was asked to be the best man at a wedding of one of his co-workers who was easily twenty-five years younger. This perplexed me. How did he relate to this young man? Maybe Dad was more voluble at work than he was at home. I attended the wedding with my parents and it was evident Dad had mentored this young man, was a role model to this young man, just as he had been to me. Love through action.

Timing

Finalizing the timing will be a trial and error process at this point. Make adjustments and retest the car. You will want to advance the ignition as much as possible while avoiding engine ping or knock. This is technically known as "pre-detonation," and can be very harmful to an engine. Detonation happens when the timing is so far advanced that the gasoline air mixture ignites with a full force before the piston is near the top of its cylinder. A significant loss of power happens and damage to the piston and valve can occur. Detonation is easy to detect because it is accompanied by an unusual "pinging" engine sound.

The timing was wrong when Daddy died. At twenty-five, I had completed my master's degree and was living in Oregon. I was still learning how to be an adult and operate in a world far from home. For a while I lost the ability to restore my equilibrium, to keep my engine running strong. My heart was pinging erratically. I careened from boyfriend to boyfriend, searching for steadiness, for someone who could teach me.

Though he's been dead for thirty-six years, I miss him every day. My father didn't live long enough to know my husband or stepsons. It is my greatest regret.

With time, I realized the gift he gave me: How to maintain a strong engine by learning on my own through trial and error. To be responsible. To show love through action. Test-drive and listen carefully for any pinging to make sure there's just the right mixture of fuel and air for optimum performance.

On Reading

I binge read like my dad smoked Winstons. He lit each new cigarette from the one burning to ashes in his fingertips. I am on the final chapter in one book and have the next book lined up bedside so I can quickly grab it and not waste a moment of indecision about what to read next. In fact, I know what I'll be reading for the next six months if I continue with my goal of finishing three books a month. Although if I keep buying four books a month, the math story-problem doesn't have a tidy solution. It means the books keep piling up on my bed headboard.

In fact, it's become dangerous. A book launched itself onto my head the other night while I was asleep. Thankfully, it was a thin paperback, so no lasting damage occurred. It startled the hell out of me, though. I grabbed George's hand and said "What was that?" Mid-snore he squeezed my hand and said clearly "It's okay" and promptly went back to sleep. Wouldn't you know it? The book was *The Kind of Brave You Wanted to Be*, by Brian Doyle; a sign that Doyle is just as mischievous from the beyond as he was alive. It reminded me of when I was a little girl and my pet hamster escaped his cage. My sister and mother and I looked all day throughout the house but couldn't find him. That night my mom woke with a scream—Hammie had run across her face as she slept! I was directed to find Hammie a new home.

The first time I binge-read, it was my mother's fault.

At bedtime when I was a child, my mother would read me the beloved Madeline books by Ludwig Bemelmans, over and over again. We owned every book Bemelmans wrote. My favorite was *Madeline's Rescue*. So foreign to think about little girls living in Paris.

When I still needed to hold my mom's hand to cross the street, she started taking my sister and me to the Canoga Park branch library in Los Angeles every week. I loved going to the library. I would sit on the floor in the cozy children's section and inhale Beatrix Potter's Peter Rabbit books. What made them special was they fit in my small hands. Everything was miniaturized to fit these tiny animals. Mr. Jeremy Fisher who fashioned a boat out of a lily pad and set off to fish for minnows. Then it was on to *The Borrowers* and *The Borrowers Afield* and all their adventures. I delighted in the miniature world they inhabited.

Once I'd picked out all the books I wanted to take home, I stacked them up with the smallest books on top and handed the stack to the woman who sat behind the date-stamp machine. The limit was ten books. The *chunk-chunk* the machine made when the librarian stamped the card that fit into the neat little slot at the front of each book was such an affirming, solid sound. It meant escape into other worlds.

In grade school I moved on to Carolyn Keene, doyenne of the young adult mystery series. I could easily get lost in Nancy Drew's latest adventure. It turns out Carolyn Keene wasn't an author at all but a pseudonym created by publisher Edward Stratemeyer.

My mom, sister, and I all shared books and the pleasure of reading. We all read Mary Stewart's books and Agatha Christie's books, which created a common language. Somehow your pleasure gets doubled when you can recommend a good book to a friend.

I binged Pam Houston when I was single and longed

to have as many exciting lovers as she had and travel even half as much as she did. Her love for her dogs resonated deeply with me.

Reading has always been important to me, and it's not about the quality of what I read. My literary lexicon ranges across many genres. It's more about quantity. I love learning, and the more I read, the more I know. Or at least I like to think so. I devour books in whale-like gulps. Open mouth, insert krill. Open brain, insert book.

Most recently I found a new favorite author after reading *A Homemade Life* and was disappointed to learn she's written only three books. I'm waiting for your next one, Molly Wizenberg. I just recently read that her podcast, *Spilled Milk,* is taking up most of her time now. Right before Molly, I binged Ruth Reichl's delicious food stories, which made me want to be a food critic just like her. I've read everything John Daniel has written. He's local and it makes me feel like I know him.

For a while I was on a Robert B. Parker mystery binge, then on to James Lee Burke and his evocative mystery series set in Louisiana. Before those two authors, Sue Grafton's twenty-five novels, the alphabetically titled series that began in 1982 with *A is for Alibi,* kept me engaged for years. And before Sue, orchid-raising detective Nero Wolfe occupied a large amount of my reading attention.

Last summer right before we left on vacation to the East Coast, I was excited to see that Anne Tyler had come out with a new book. I read *Clock Dance* on the flight to Baltimore. I love airplane trips, especially long ones when time is liminal and reading is uninterrupted. Tyler's *Dinner at the Homesick Restaurant* is a favorite of mine. *Breathing Lessons* is another book of Tyler's that I savored. That woman can't write a bad book. Although I did struggle a bit with *A Spool of Blue Thread.*

I am a bookseller's best friend. Acquiring books makes me feel rich. And sharing them makes me feel positively wealthy. I love the little free libraries. When we were on a wine tasting vacation in Carlton, Oregon, I scored *After the Ecstasy the Laundry,* by Jack Kornfield, in the little free library near the town square. When traveling, I always leave a book I've finished either on the plane, in the Airbnb where we've stayed, or in a little free library, if I manage to find one. I've stashed copies of my memoir, *Homespun,* in several little free libraries around my hometown.

Reading brings me much pleasure. It's not that I needed to escape into other worlds because my childhood was lacking in some way. It was a bonus of my childhood that I had time to read. I wasn't required to take care of a younger sibling because I was the youngest. I didn't feel any pressure to help bring in income. Neither sports nor music competed for my time because academics were stressed above all else. We didn't go to the movies. I read. I read for entertainment. I read to metaphorically travel. I read to understand life beyond the insular world of my childhood. I think reading is what led me to writing.

Many authors have opened worlds to me. I want to do the same. I want young people to know what it was like to grow up in the early 1960s. And I want the stories I write to resonate with sixty-year-olds through shared childhood memories. I just finished *The Art of Memoir* by Mary Karr and it was spot on.

In my "seeking" phase, I read everything by Anne Lamott. Her message of hope and mercy from outside the walls of a church was instrumental in building my empathy skills.

During my early years as a feminist, I read everything Rita Mae Brown wrote. After *Rubyfruit Jungle,* however, I struggled to make the switch to her Sneaky Pie Brown mystery series.

I recently devoured Dani Shapiro's memoirs. They showed me how to be completely honest in my writing.

In retirement, I realize that a lot of my volunteer commitments center around literacy. I serve on the board of Springfield Young Readers, a local chapter of the Dolly Parton Imagination Library. This nonprofit gets books into the hands of children ages birth to five years old and encourages parents to read to their children so these children are poised for success when they enter kindergarten. I was a volunteer reader through the Start Making a Reader Today program.

I know that being a big reader can lead to a fuller, richer life. Being a voracious reader made me a quick learner, because it helped me make connections and hold two disparate ideas simultaneously in my brain. Reading taught me how to write—key to my successful career as a planner because I had to know how to write land-use plans. Reading taught me how to be an editor of others' writing and learn what makes a memo sing. In my role as an executive director, being well-read helped me write speeches that were compelling and called people to action.

There is nothing better than having a book conversation with someone at a party and learning about a new author. It makes my brain synapses rub their hands together in glee. Best party greeting ever: What are you reading? I'm always open to recommendations.

Both/And

My first act of resistance as a young adult was to apply to the environmental studies program at the University of California at Santa Barbara (UCSB). I needed to be pushed out of my comfort zone, learn how to open out. My dad was bewildered by my choice of a college that didn't have a football team and of a major that wasn't math or engineering. All through high school I had been on a trajectory to declare a college major in hard science—math or marine biology.

I was raised by risk-averse parents who were kids during the Depression and survived by eating onion sandwiches. They moved to California from Colorado Springs, and both worked in the shipyards during World War II. The advice I received was all about taking responsibility: Get your education so you have opportunities. Don't mess up. Stay focused. Always take the straight and narrow rather than the meandering path. Growing up, my life was all about either/or. About closing in rather than opening up. About drawing self-restrictive boxes around myself.

As I entered college more than forty years ago, I wondered: Does our approach to the environment—or for that matter, life itself—always have to be an either/or option or can it be both/and? Can we push ourselves to think in terms of expansive consonance, rather than limit our thinking to reductive clichés? As we celebrate the fiftieth anniversary of the environmental studies program at

UCSB, these concepts resonate even louder.

I grew up in a Los Angeles suburb, and by the time I left for college my senses were stunted. The surrounding landscape was devoid of the wild. When I moved to the beach, I began to awaken: listening for the foghorn that helped guide ships through the foggy Santa Barbara Channel, watching the shorebirds forage for crabs, and seeing the exuberant orange nasturtium blossoms invade any unplanted space. Starting to appreciate nature's smells and sounds.

I was seventeen when I arrived at UCSB. Unformed, eager to be transformed, I entered the lecture hall of my first undergraduate class. Hundreds of students sat ready to be convinced—to have their ways of thinking pushed and challenged. It was 1976 and the environmental studies program was still young, formed in response to escalating threats to the environment, specifically the 1969 Santa Barbara oil spill. It was the beginning of my adult life.

I wanted to occupy Professor Barry Schuyler's brain and let his wisdom and knowledge seep into my sunburned skin. I loved the way he differentiated between wants and needs. Can we want only what we need? His course included an optional field trip sailing the Cassandra across the Santa Barbara Channel to the Channel Islands. Of course I went, I had never been sailing before. We dropped anchor in a small cove on Santa Cruz Island, twenty-eight miles off shore. The sky was overcast with a faint glimmer of sun.

I was smitten with Paul, one of the students on board. Paul put on his wetsuit, flippers, and snorkel and casually dropped into the water. Paul dove for abalone. Its harvest had not yet been regulated by law. Making several shallow dives, Paul pried the abalone off the rocks and swam them up to those of us on board. Barry cleaned them, cut them into steaks, and pounded them flat, grilling them to perfection. Of course I ate them, I'd never tasted abalone before. I was drunk on the idea that I could be a student and an adventurer. That I could be more than one thing. Both/and.

Paul lived in an Airstream trailer in Isla Vista. No squeezing four roommates into a two-bedroom apartment for him. He was getting an Environmental Studies degree, maintaining a vegetable garden, and parenting a mutt. He was present in his life; no either/or. I felt like a ripe peach. Soft, ready to burst. If someone had bit into me, I would drip juice. I kept finding reasons to visit his space, picking sweet cherry tomatoes from his garden and playing with his hound, Cosmo. He took a heavy load of classes spring and fall terms and skipped every winter term to drive his VW bus to Baja to surf. Scholar and surfer. Both/and.

One of the more memorable conversations I recall with my dad in my first year of college occurred when I was describing to him the transect analysis we were conducting in class. We'd lay a grid on the ground and then count every type of plant and animal we observed. He said, "What are you going to do with that degree? Count snails for the rest of your life?" I know now that it was his loving way of saying I'm worried you'll end up unemployable and poor. (That did not happen.)

An overpowering scent of eucalyptus and salt air, which I will forever associate with exhilarating metamorphosis, permeated the campus and Isla Vista. In seminars I inhaled information about how storm events loaded creeks with large woody debris and improved the pool habitat so salmonids could gain girth and strength for their journey to the ocean. I reveled in this riverine knowledge taught by forest geomorphology Professor Ed Keller that I could see play out on field trips. In other classes I acquired knowledge about bioregionalism and the carrying capacity of Earth.

I was newly alive those four years at UCSB, high on life-altering moments that I didn't recognize at the time.

I learned how to measure the impact of industrialization through life-cycle cost accounting and broadened my mind to embrace the notion of the interdependence of all our collective actions.

I attended a consciousness-raising circle where we focused on the systemic injustices against women by the patriarchy. I filled myself with Shulamith Firestone, Kate Millet, and Betty Friedan. I became outraged. My mom suggested I read "nice murder mysteries" instead of books that made me sputter. I took a work-study job at the women's center on campus and became righteous but confused, not wanting to give up men to become a feminist. Either/or. I wanted to embrace men for what their bodies could do and for their clumsy attempts at wooing. I started to think about both/and. I am a feminist AND I love men. We can be multitudes.

I tried to grasp the impacts of my actions on the environment and to reconcile the either/or of loving fashion and being a consumer with the frugality of environmentalism. I learned that shopping at vintage and used clothing stores could be virtuous rather than a stigma of being poor. I adopted the mantra of conscious consumption—reduce, reuse, repurpose. I struggled with the cognitive dissonance of both/and—of holding two disparate ideas in my brain at the same time. I am passionate about caring for the environment AND I am a clothes horse.

On those searching, magical mornings when I walked the beach before the fog burned off, I extended my thoughts to push beyond either/or reductionist thinking. My universe was enlarging exponentially as new neural pathways formed in my brain. My ecological compassion expanded through direct experience of the living world, which until then had been limited to my mother's flower garden and summer camping trips in the Sierras.

Both/and. Reconciling the idea that there is more than one way to do something, more than one way to think about something. One does not eclipse the other. Both can be right and righteous. I'm still learning, but the environmental studies program gave me a tremendous head start. The environmental studies program gave me knowledge to be a good environmental citizen and gave me tools to help change the world.

(This recollection is dedicated to environmental studies professors and mentors: Jeff Dozier, Ed Keller, Mel Manalis, Marc McGinnis, Roderick Nash, Orin and Cindy Sage, Barry Schuyler, and Paul Wack. Thanks for blowing my mind.)

Sewing Frenzy

I was broke and selling my plasma to help pay for packages of ramen. I desperately needed a job. As I perused the wants ads I saw a posting for a seamstress at McKenzie Bend, a manufacturer of women's clothing in Eugene, Oregon. My skill set was limited, but I learned how to sew by watching my mother, who was an accomplished self-taught seamstress and pattern maker. Her ability to make anything I could dream up taught me to be a clothes horse at a young age. I mailed in my resumé, telling them I had been sewing since age twelve.

I got called to come in for an interview. I entered a huge warehouse, where at least a hundred women, heads bent over their sewing machines, frantically stitched jeans. A deep thrumming reverberated through the high-ceiling room. Fine cotton lint coated the concrete floor. Pattern pieces lay stacked head high by each machine. Barely contained mania filled the space. Jeans extruded from the industrial-grade machines at an astonishing speed. A brisk-walking woman led me into a room off to the side for my interview. I almost turned around and walked out. No way could I keep up with that kind of automaton-like movement. I wanted to use my brain.

I had invested so much time in my education and had nearly finished the master's degree that conferred serious smarts. I didn't want to let my parents down by not completing my degree after they had sacrificed their time and money to help me have the opportunity an advanced degree would allow. Getting this degree wasn't just about me. It was an homage to Mom and Dad.

I would be working with women who had little opportunity and little education to fall back on. Completing my degree would mean I was lucky enough to be in a position to leave this rote labor behind. I had to stuff my petty classist thoughts and let the lure of a paycheck fuel my desperation to succeed in this interview.

The interview was in the room where they made prototypes for each new piece of clothing that would be introduced that season. I was handed seven pieces of denim fabric and a zipper and told to make a pair of shorts.

When I worked at a fabric store in high school, I earned extra money by sewing samples that the owner would display to inspire the home sewer. I had a deadline for each piece, but no one watched me make it. If I flubbed and had to rip out a seam and redo it, no one was the wiser.

For this interview I needed to look like I knew what I was doing. I laid the pieces of fabric out on a table and decided to start with the zipper. I was accustomed to sewing machines powered by a foot pedal, but these had a paddle you pressed with your thigh. I had no way to calibrate the pressure from my thigh. Sewing with that machine was like driving a Maserati when you were used to a Toyota.

It was my first time using an overlock machine. The threads locked the raw edges together and the extra fabric was cut off by a knife that ran alongside the needle. I had to watch out for my fingers as the fabric raced away from me under the pressure foot. I could barely breathe. The silence felt oppressive, interrupted only by the staccato bursts of *rrrrrrrrr* emanating from my machine.

Somehow, miraculously, I completed the shorts in the time they had allotted. The leg diameters didn't match because the seams had uneven amounts of fabric knifed off as they ran under the needle. A person would never actually be able to wear the shorts. The waistband barely managed to encircle the circumference of the waist. But I held them up triumphantly, amazed that they resembled a pair of shorts and that my fingers were intact.

I got the job as a prototype maker. I created blouses and pants under the moniker "Frenzy," which tells you a little bit about our timeline. The pattern designer would cut out fabric pieces and leave them at my sewing station, along with her drawing of what the garment should look like.

Every morning I made something new. One day, it was a plaid shirt. The next day a pair of jeans with no waistband—the new cool thing at the time. I never did understand how they decided what designs would sell and could be sent into production and what designs to eliminate. I got to keep everything that didn't go into production. This free wardrobe of jeans and shirts was a bonus for a clothes-horse graduate student with no money.

I researched and wrote my thesis at night after sewing all day. Finishing my degree has allowed me a life of privilege—using my hands AND my brain to better the world.

Collecting and Recollecting

Rocks on the end table. Bird nests on the kitchen counter. Shells on the sideboard. Bird feathers in a dining room vase. Sand dollars on the window sill. Dried sage bundles on the mantle. In my writing area I have marble from Greece, pink granite from the South Dakota hills, and serpentine from the McKenzie River. A heart-shaped rock collection threatening to take over every inch of counter space in the downstairs bathroom. Keeping my mother near through my collections.

I don't think it's unusual to decorate with nature because Mom's décor of choice was Early American rockhound. The familiarity of having rocks in the living room is anchoring, calming. Every time we went on vacation, Mom collected rocks notable for their color or configuration. Dad affectionately complained that the camper was so weighted down, we wouldn't get over Yosemite's Tioga Pass to get home.

Mom landscaped with rocks as well. Dry creek beds meandered throughout her iris bed in the backyard and the shade garden in the front yard. It made sense for a yard with no rain in the desiccating Los Angeles basin.

My mom's rating criterion for a place to spend time: "Does it have good rocks?" was superfluous because she could always find good rocks. Why did my mom have such affection for rocks? She was a collector. And she had an artistic eye. Maybe it was like a treasure hunt for her.

Once, when we were camping, she found an arrowhead along the Lake Cachuma shore. She was always paying attention. Her one sister, fifteen years her elder, was married to a geologist. He worked in the mine near Cripple Creek, Colorado. I suspect when my mom visited them, rocks were a prominent topic of conversation. Maybe they even decorated their house with rocks.

Right after my dad died, when Mom was sixty-two, I asked her to come visit me in Oregon. We drove to the Warm Springs Indian Reservation hotel where I thought she would appreciate the beautiful rocks in rim-rock country and wide open space, away from everything that reminded her of Dad. What I didn't bargain for was the fact that because it was Indian territory, we couldn't remove rocks. Major error on my part. Mom was disappointed but philosophical about it. We headed south and took a boat trip on the Rogue River and wandered around during the lunch break looking for rocks.

Bringing the outside in is an important concept to me. Integrating the natural and constructed worlds allows me to feel like I'm living with nature. I spent much of my growing up years playing outdoors—swimming, bicycling, making mud pies as pioneers, hide-and-seek, kick-the-can—the weather was always perfect for outdoor play in Los Angeles. As a young girl, I found it impossible to resist the call of the outside world on a beautiful day, with its aroma of honeysuckle and sun-baked asphalt. Our vacations were focused outdoors as well—camping and fishing in the Sierras. We weren't the kind of family to go to museums, the theater, or ballet. Nature was our touchstone. We were Forest Bathing long before anyone coined the term. When we walked through the forest, we inhaled the resinous aroma of pine duff and listened for the tiny red-breasted nuthatch. Dried needles crackled underfoot. We looked for monkey flower and foxglove.

Colllecting and Recollecting

I always enjoyed the outdoor field trips for my college environmental studies classes. We would head to the Channel Islands to study endemic plant species or to avocado orchards to measure out transects and count all the plants and animals within each section. We backpacked along rivers to observe the impact of large, woody debris on river health, learning to understand that pools and riffles and side channel habitat for fish were created by the dynamics of flooding events. This habitat allowed fish to mature and thrive.

I still thrive outdoors. Walking on a beach, tending my garden, camping, observing bird life. My best moments are when I feel rooted in nature. An early introduction to rocks and lakes and streams, to flowers and feathers, has kept me grounded. My parents taught me to appreciate bringing in the outside.

In a vacation rental on the northeastern reach of the Tasmanian coast, I am suddenly beset with an almost bodily sense of being in my childhood backyard. In the front yard of the vacation rental, iris are planted in a bed of small colorful stones, just like in the backyard where I grew up. Mom has been gone fourteen years now. Whenever I travel, I carry a baggie filled with her ashes and leave some of her in places with beautiful rocks and gardens. I had scattered Mom's ashes at the base of each iris when we arrived. Overnight the iris opened. I can almost hear Mom exclaiming over their beauty and pocketing a few rocks to take home with her. I know she is here with me. I run down the stairs to the beach, and soon I am happily lost in the hunt, head bent over as if in supplication. Choosing some rocks and discarding others, mindful of the weight limit for my baggage on the long flight home.

Reunion Reflections

When my sister Sallie turned sixty this year, she decided it was time to explore the American contingent of our father's Greek family. Our dad died when he was sixty-four, adding a sense of urgency to her mission. Colorado Springs, Colorado was the obvious venue. That's where my dad and his siblings all grew up.

Three generations of cousins gathered for a first-ever family reunion: seven first cousins, six second cousins, and four third cousins, ages four to sixty-nine. All of our respective parents are gone. I hadn't seen some of my cousins in fifty years. But they, like me, were pulled by this force of connecting—an opportunity to spend time reflecting on our parents' lives.

In 1908 at age seventeen, my dad's father, Vasillios Konstantine Papaspyridis, emigrated to the United States from Kandyla, Greece. His last name was shortened to Pappas at Ellis Island. Most everyone called him Pappy. Along with thousands of other Greeks looking for work in the gold mines, railroads, and steel mills, he settled in Colorado Springs forty-five miles north of Pueblo, Colorado. Pueblo in the early 1900s was the center for one of the most dynamic and viable Greek communities in the West. In 1905 the Greek Orthodox Community Association of Pueblo was formed. The association had three goals: build a church, secure and maintain cemetery facilities, and help Greeks settle in the region. Fifteen thousand Greeks were said to be in Colorado between 1900 and 1920.

Pappy married Zelma Lillie in 1915 and they had four children. My dad and his three siblings—the Pappas Four—all grew up in Colorado Springs. Dad's big brother Denny was born in 1916, Dad in 1919, then Billie and Gordon in 1921 and 1924, respectively. They were the first Pappas generation to be born in the United States. As was the case for many immigrants, assimilation was extremely important to Pappy. No Greek was spoken at home and his children did not attend the Greek Orthodox Church. Pappy owned a restaurant, The Gold Nugget, in downtown Colorado Springs. The Gold Nugget was a hub in the community and turned out to be important to the future of the Pappas Four. Three of the four met their spouses while working at the restaurant.

As we're sharing anecdotes, cousin Pam recalls her dad, Denny, saying that Pappy felt strongly that it was important to keep the family together after Zelma died when the kids were young. There was shared chuckling when we all realized that when a stubborn Pappas makes a decision, there's no sense in arguing. By sheer will, Pappy worked sixteen-hour days in the restaurant and raised four children. Once Pappy made his decision, I suspect he had high expectations that all four children would carry their fair share of the load. I suspect this was all unspoken, as so many things in my family were.

Everyone met up at the house we'd rented for the reunion in Colorado Springs. Later that evening we ate at the Golden Bee, one of the iconic Broadmoor Resort restaurants. Our agenda for the three-day trip was packed. The sites we chose to visit during our reunion united us around places that were important to our parents.

Friday morning was dedicated to nostalgia. First we drove to the house where the Pappas Four grew up, which is now dilapidated and guarded by three large German shepherds. We drove past The Gold Nugget (now, ironically, a Vietnamese restaurant as new immigrants have moved to Colorado Springs). Only my two cousins who still live in Colorado Springs had memories of seeing Pappy cook in the restaurant. We made photo stops at the elementary, junior high, and high schools that all four kids attended and at Evergreen Cemetery, where Pappy and Zelma are buried.

We had 1:20 p.m. tickets for the Pikes Peak Cog Railway, the highest cog railroad in the world, reaching 14,115 feet. Pikes Peak stands alone at the eastern front of Colorado's mountain ranges. I remember Mom and Dad talking about watching the race car drivers challenge each other and the mountain in the Pikes Peak Hill Climb.

At the summit, the view to the west is the Continental Divide, to the east is Colorado Springs and Garden of the Gods. The southern panorama includes the Sangre de Cristo mountains. So inspirational was the view from Pikes Peak to one traveler, English teacher Katherine Lee Bates, that she immortalized it in the poem *America the Beautiful*.

Following the three-hour round trip, we drove back to our vacation house through the ethereal red sandstone formations in Garden of the Gods city park. I'm sorry we ran out of time to see "the grandest mile of scenery in Colorado—Seven Falls."

A benefit of vacationing in Colorado Springs is the ever-present wildlife. On a Saturday morning walk, cousin Gerrie and I spied three six-point bucks foraging in a neighbor's garden, closely watched by a coyote who was mobbed by a tidings of angry magpies.

Following our walk, all the cousins took off for Canon City, where we boarded the 11:30 a.m. Royal Gorge Railroad dining car for lunch and a trip through the 1,200-foot-deep Arkansas River canyon.

Saturday night was discovery time. We shared family

photos and penciled in dates along a table-size timeline that Pam created. We toasted our Greek heritage with ouzo, celebrated Pappy's resilience in keeping the family together after Zelma died, and commented on how much our parents would have loved to see us all together.

I was hoping to hear a family story that would explain this endless need of mine to make a difference; to come to some sense of peace with this underlying urgency that drives me. Why I can't just be retired in my retirement. Why I have this obsessive need to save the elephants. Recycle. Protect special lands. Fundraise to house the homeless. Feed the hungry. Take back the night. Fight for the underdog. Maybe it's as simple as Pappy manifesting himself in my life.

Sunday morning, a group of cousins hiked in Ute Valley Park. Then Sallie, my nephew Alexander, and I took a twenty-minute drive to Manitou Springs. And just like my parents did more than seventy years ago, we shopped for Navajo turquoise and filled our bottles with carbonated mineral spring water that originates from snowmelt in the Rockies. Each of the springs that line the main street tastes different. We liked the flavor of Stratton Spring the best.

From our conversations, I learned that none of our Pappas parents were talkers; it wasn't just a characteristic peculiar to Dad. This tendency toward reticence, combined with how young the Pappas Four were when their mom died, is why there are few family stories.

From pictures, I surmised that the nose many of us share is inherited from Zelma.

The strong work ethic and the drive for higher education that runs deep and broad across all Pappas generations comes from Pappy. Of the thirteen Pappas cousins old enough to have graduated from high school, I counted twenty-two advanced degrees.

Even two generations later, Pappy defines us all. We are the children of immigrants.

Livestock Lessons in Leadership

I've learned a lot about leadership by living on a farm, wrangling cows. The simple lessons from the farm have served me well in my role as CEO of various nonprofit agencies. And vice versa. The other day as I was scrubbing the kitchen sink to get the house presentable for a dinner party, I looked out the window onto the wet, pewter day and my Cow CEO role kicked in.

Identify the Nature of the Problem

"There's a cow in the yard! It's not ours," I holler to George. I have to jar him out of his focused concentration at the stove. Usually when one cow gets out, others follow. And we had a bull in our pasture that was looking for love. George was deep in the throes of making langoustine cardinal and maque choux for our Mardi Gras-themed meal. The aroma of browning onions filled the kitchen. The windows were steamed up from the bubbling saucepan filled with langoustine. Everything was timed perfectly for the arrival of our guests.

Be Ready to Jump into the Fray with Energy and Optimism

"Are you at a stopping point?" I yelled as I rushed to pull on my knee-high Boggs over my clean-the-house outfit. I raced out the door to face the unpredictable bovine while George turned the stove down to simmer. *Leaders must have the confidence to enter deeply into the fray and make a decision in the midst of ambiguity.*

Contain the Problem

I headed out in the drumming rain toward the sodden garden patch to cut the twelve-hundred-pound heifer off from doing further damage to our lawn with her heavy hoofs.

Wouldn't you know it? Our irrepressible young bull, whom we had planned to castrate earlier that day, frolicked alongside the heifer, separated only by the pasture fence, bellowing his high-pitched baby bull language. He was thinking, "I outsmarted them. I'm going to have my shot while I've still got it."

We'd called off the castration because the saturated soil made it too slippery and unsafe to maneuver him into the squeeze chute. *Leaders keep the crew's safety in the forefront of decision-making.*

I successfully cut the heifer off by raising my arms to the heavens. She stared at me in wild alarm, but I got her to turn around by lowering my left arm in the direction I wanted her to move. I walked purposefully behind her, just off her left flank where she could still see me out of the corner of her eye. Cows do not like to be blindsided. *Leadership is about respecting the individual and understanding her predilection.*

Determine How the Problem Originated

By that time, George had punched our neighbor's number into his cell phone to ask if he owned a white-faced heifer. We didn't want to herd the animal back to the wrong neighbor's field. Neighbor Larry conceded yes, he did, but he was in Palm Springs and unable to assist. Ahh, Palm Springs. My mind floated toward the scene. Sunny. Blue sky. Poolside, reading a book. The tang of sunscreen in the air.

I snapped back to reality when the heifer stopped short at the fence separating our property from Larry's. Then she proceeded to walk right through the loosened barb wire. The tangled mess functioned more as an open gate than a barrier at that moment. A hole in the fence that did not appear to be cow-size expanded with her passage.

Craft a Solution

Although the initial problem was fixed, we had to repair the hole or the same problem would occur again. After we quickly conferred, George hustled off to the barn to retrieve two metal T-posts and I went to the garden shed to get the heavy metal post driver. We met at the shop to gather clips into a bucket; we picked up a pair of pliers, trotted back out to the fence, and prayed that nothing in the kitchen was burning. *Leaders must be cognizant that fixing one problem sometimes creates another.*

Execute the Solution as a Team to Create Investment in the Outcome

The drenching rain had morphed into hail as we bent over to drive the posts into the ground and clip the fencing to the posts. We could only laugh at this point. It took us almost an hour to corral the cow and fix the fence. Our schedule was shot, we were soaking wet, and we still had to find a way to recover and serve our guests an edible meal.

Find the Serendipity

Just then a soft, far-off *karoo karoo* carried through the air, pausing our work. High overhead, a hundred sandhill cranes flew in an uneven V formation with a long trailing end. Their wings beat gracefully through the air and we were grateful that we were outside at that moment. *A leader recognizes that problems are often opportunities in disguise.*

File the Report

Dinner turned out a bit well-done, but we had a good story to share with our guests.

My Life Is Not *Mingle* Magazine

Mingle magazine's masthead reads "creative ideas for unique gatherings." The very thought fills me with glee. I hoard *Mingle* magazine issues like they are the Holy Grail.

In my dreams, my life is a series of staged events with compliant friends, made to look effortless. Everything is perfect, nothing is left to fate. Nostalgic beach picnics with real wicker baskets. Glamping playdates with Airstream trailers parked in our pasture with vintage tablecloths on Formica tabletops. A backyard bash where everything is color-coordinated and the mole hills are under control. Dinner parties where the menu is spelled out on chalkboard, with a "farmhouse" theme and not just because it's taking place on our farm. Girlfriend get-togethers where we all create outrageous jewelry and wear matching pashmina scarves. Cupcake-tasting date nights. A seaside champagne campfire with s'mores. Backyard wine tastings with sugar cookies that spell out the wine names. Everyone has a good time and thinks the hostess is amazing. Maybe I don't need to be that hostess. I just need to be invited to one of these amazing gatherings. I would happily be a compliant guest at someone else's event.

My husband scoffs at all this pretend. From his perspective, the food is the event. Anything else is just packaging. I think the packaging is what makes it all deliciously fun.

I want to know if all this perfection that I see in the pages of *Mingle* brings happiness. I attempt to find out by throwing a themed party. It is a champagne tasting event: a big splurge. We share four magnums of L'Ermitage Roederer, a vertical tasting from 1998, 2002, 2006, and 2012 vintages. We invite four couples who are champagne aficionados. I buy printed tasting notes. The night of the party, we line up the champagne magnums on the kitchen island in perfect military order, by year disgorged. The appetizers are artfully displayed on the table. The table is set with matching hors d'oeuvre plates, forks, and napkins. We ask our wine-making friend to open each bottle, describe the champagne, and let guests taste and make notes. In a burst of excitement, he opens all four bottles at once and people start to drink. Any sense of decorum is quickly abandoned. The delicate gougeres are consumed immediately, champagne glasses get mixed up, and the smoked mussels are inhaled. George cannot fry French fries in truffle oil fast enough to meet demand. I am frustrated that no one pauses to make tasting notes. The Rule Girl in me wants everyone to follow the instructions. Who knew eight adults could be so undisciplined?

I find out via a flurry of emails the following day that everyone who attended loved the exuberance of the event and the yummy food. Tasting notes be damned.

Maybe that's what I like about the *Mingle* vignettes—everyone is orderly, even the four-year-olds dressed like pirates who wait until given permission to dip into the booty of gold doubloon-colored donuts hanging on spray-painted white peg board.

Do I want to make my life a "work of art"? Maybe. On some days. On other days I'm content to wild around the farm with unkempt hair, wearing the same clothes I've worn for a week.

The reality of my life often doesn't match my imagination, or as my girlfriends and I often lament, "I like the idea, it's the execution that lacks." I like the idea of matching and cleanliness and newness. A coffee table and end tables that match. Sheets with a matching coverlet. Space in the refrigerator, unused, clean, and brilliant white, instead of shelves crammed with Tupperware containers with three teaspoons of mystery meat and moldy sour cream.

Since I'm a Libra, I can't think of one way without acknowledging the other. The thing and its opposite. In theory, my mind stays balanced.

If we weren't savers and recyclers, we would be wasteful, and that is criminal. I love that virtuous feeling of making do with less. In the summer months I revel in tallying how many weeks we can eat from the vegetable garden without buying grocery store vegetables. And how many cold showers we can take outside without consuming hot water. I recycle magazines by giving them to health clinics. Recycling is not a tidy thing. There are stacks of cardboard boxes, barrels of glass, boxes of paper, and a container of metal.

The problem is we have too much physical space on the farm, which makes it easy for stuff to accumulate. But when it starts to take up too much psychic space, I announce it's time to go to the dump, where we do most of our recycling. I don't think the people featured in *Mingle* magazine are recyclers, nor does frugality seem a consideration. Otherwise, how would everything match and look so new, even in its vintageness?

At the dump we drop off our recyclables in their respective areas. One day, as we are disposing of champagne bottles (a possible theme emerging here?), a man parks his pickup right behind ours and starts unloading cases of empty wine bottles. George can't take his eyes off the pristine white boxes and clean empty bottles and is immediately at the man's side. We make our own wine, which requires lots of empty wine bottles. The man explains that he is from a local winery where people can bottle their own wine and he is recycling unused bottles. George asks if he can take the cases. Instead of ridding ourselves of accumulated detritus, we come home with eleven cases of bottles. George grins as though he has scored a major coup. I shake my head in futile exasperation.

My driver's side car window is permanently in the up position because the motor to raise and lower it is broken. I have blue tape over the raising/lowering mechanism as a memory trigger so I DO NOT LOWER THE CAR WINDOW. Otherwise I have to grip the window between both palms and forcibly inch it back up to close. The dealership repair quote is three hundred dollars. Instead, George promises to repair it. Six months later I still have to get out of my car to speak to the gas attendant when I fill up. In Oregon, it's against the law to fill up your own gas tank.

The zipper to the coin compartment of my wallet will only open wide enough to allow a quarter to emerge after much shaking and squeezing, usually in front of a retail clerk with a line of customers waiting. I can't bring myself to toss the wallet just because the zipper broke. The shaking and squeezing ritual unfolds every time I need to access change.

I have spent the morning cleaning the oven's interior from too many overflowing apple pies. The oven is forty-four years old and has a self-cleaning mechanism that is broken. Why spend fifteen hundred dollars to replace a good oven when I can "self-clean" it myself?

The accommodations I make in my daily life don't strike me as odd. They are my stab at frugality. They are not orchestrated perfection. They are not wicker baskets at a seaside picnic. I don't dare bring *The Life-Changing Magic of Tidying Up* into this house because George would be afraid I would throw out perfectly decent stuff. Decluttering is not a word that resonates with him. I imagine my friends with higher tidiness quotients are secretly disgusted, so I distract them by gifting them with new things I've made.

These new things are repurposed from old things we have on the farm: bag dryers and napkin rings from fallen trees, birdhouses from old fence posts, wind chimes from bent irrigation pipe, and prayer flags and patchwork pillows from fabric scraps. Predictably, every time we're able to use something from the shop, George says, "See, that's why you should never throw anything away!"

Here is what one friend recently said about the Christmas gifts we make each year. "Thanks to you my onions and peppers traveled home safely, cinched into their soft, white mesh bags. What a great gift. Our house is filled with your creations! At the grocery store yesterday, after the young cashier commented on my new bags I found myself excitedly listing all the Pappas/Grier gifts we've received over the years. I was babbling a hundred words a second: baggie dryer, draft stopper, windchimes, ice masher, chocolate hazelnuts, wooden box, notecards. Then I saw the line behind me and the flashing screen waiting for my signature and the polite smile pasted on the cashier's face. I quickly exited but I'm sure those people behind me were so very jealous of our new vegetable bags!"

Our grown sons have given up on us. After asking several times why one of our living room chair's ripped leather has never been reupholstered, our oldest quit asking when I said it never made it to the top of the spend list. They tease me and their dad about things we've owned since they were kids, forty years ago. Our stereo system and speakers are so outdated they are now vintage. Our bedroom curtains desperately need replacing. I get stymied by a failure of reconciliation between having and frugaling, between buying and using what we have.

Yet I still like to dream that someday, as though stepping into the pages of *Mingle*, someone will surprise me and invite me to a themed creative gathering in my honor. The invitation will arrive in the mail, written in cursive. I will be told to wear a dress of vintage lace and deep purple high-top Vans that match all the guests' shoes. I will be instructed to bring my best Motown singing voice. There will be a flash mob to Aretha's "Pink Cadillac" and everyone will know the steps.

I hope I don't have to wait too long.

Cooking Up Compassion

George has loved to cook since he worked in his frat house kitchen, under the tutelage of Cora, a strapping African-American who made magic with a limited budget. She could make a turkey last all week through careful planning. Monday's menu was turkey slices, mashed potatoes, and greens; Tuesday's was turkey gravy on open-faced sandwiches; Wednesday's was turkey enchiladas; Thursday was chili night, stretching the turkey with potatoes and beans; and Friday's was turkey and rice soup.

George has cooked all his life: through single parenthood, during his full-time farming days, while employed as a stock broker, and finally in retirement. Now in his early seventies, George cooks for a cause. He joined a group of cooks who make paella for fundraisers that support our local food bank, raise money to build tiny houses for the homeless, and fund children's services at a family shelter.

Now that I'm retired, I decided to follow his lead and become a paella maker. This is a leap of faith, given my lack of epicurean skill. Ever supportive, George surprised me with a paella pan and propane cooking setup for my birthday.

Why paella? It all started when a woman living in the Canary Islands made paella for her sisters when she returned to Oregon for a visit. She learned how to make paella from her mother-in-law. Pretty soon she was cooking for her sisters' friends, and when they all got together they decided to have a party and invite folks to come eat paella and donate to FOOD for Lane County (FFLC). Fast forward thirteen years later, and the Northwest Paella Fest has become a coveted invitation-only annual soire.

A loose-knit group of thirty do-gooders and amateur chefs cooking at the annual home-grown Paella Fest have raised $140,000 for FFLC over the past thirteen years.

Making paella is simple, especially when you can walk out to your vegetable garden and pick most of the ingredients. 1) A day ahead of the event, chop all ingredients and store in the refrigerator (two hours of prep time). 2) Make chicken stock (two hours of prep time that can happen simultaneously while chopping ingredients). 3) On the day of the fundraiser, arrive a couple hours ahead of time at the site and set up your propane tank and level your paella pan. 4) Gauge when the meal needs to be served and turn on the propane an hour before. 5) Cook the chicken or chorizo or seafood in hot olive oil. 6) Add all chopped vegetables. 7) Add spices and diced tomatoes. 8) Add Arborio (or Bombo) rice and chicken stock and stir together. 9) Stop stirring, allowing ingredients to marry. 10) Turn the pan clockwise in small increments to cook evenly and produce socarrat, the crispy goodness at the bottom of the pan. 11) Turn off the propane (about fifty minutes cooking time). 12) Add edible flowers from the garden to garnish. 13) Serve with a joyous heart.

Paella is meant to be shared communally. It allows those being helped and those with the means to help a chance to interact with each other and with the chefs. As the thick aroma of paprika and cumin emanate from the bubbling paellas, stories unfold and new friendships are made. Feeding people is such an intentional act of community. It fills me with a sense of celebration to witness the generosity of community members. Full bellies and full hearts is the best combination ever.

The original Northwest Paella Fest was so much fun that it inspired the chefs to spin off other charity events. For example, the fledgling tiny houses for the homeless movement in our community—started by the Reverend Dan Bryant with First Christian Church of Eugene and other advocates for the unhoused—is fueled by the deliciousness of an annual night out at a local winery with supporters eating paella under the stars. Just four years in, our group of paella chefs has already helped raise almost $575,000, the equivalent of twenty tiny homes, making housing affordable for those with limited means. According to Bryant, "Paella in the Vineyard has been a phenomenal success and the favorite charity event of the year for many of our supporters. We could not do it without our fabulous paella chefs."

Thanks to this committed group of paella makers, a homeless family suffering the indignity and uncertainty of homelessness has permanent shelter from the Oregon rain, and those struggling with food insecurity can access food at FFLC.

I am grateful to be part of this group that makes giving such fun and creates good out of something so simple. Many thanks to the chief instigators of this paella tradition.

Love Letter to Malheur National Wildlife Refuge

George and I don't have many rituals in our lives. Our kids are grown and have created their own holiday rhythms. Our extended families don't live close. Maybe that's why this annual trip takes on such significance. Every Memorial Day weekend we pack the car with an ice chest and birding gear—spotting scope, binoculars, bird identification books—and head east three hundred miles from our farm in Springfield to Malheur National Wildlife Refuge in Oregon's high desert to witness spring migration.

The Malheur National Wildlife Refuge was originally set aside by President Theodore Roosevelt in 1908 to protect nesting egrets and other waterfowl from unregulated plume hunting (for ladies' hats). During spring migration, Malheur turns into every birder's paradise. With a great diversity of habitat, the refuge attracts more than 320 species of birds that gorge on the banquet laid out by nature. The Blitzen Valley, the most accessible portion of the refuge, contains meadows, ponds, and extensive wetlands surrounded by sage uplands and basalt rimrock. In a wet year, the mudflats rimming Malheur and Harney lakes come alive with shorebirds. Black-necked stilts—with their long, thin supermodel legs—dip their slender bills into the mud. Delicate-winged black terns whirl overhead, catching insects.

After turning south off Highway 205 toward the refuge, we see yellow-headed blackbirds perched along the barbed wire, calling out their gutteral *gronk*. Long-billed curlews and white-faced ibis can be found in the marshy fields. The background soundtrack features a nasally *follow your lea-der* from the red-winged blackbirds.

But I'm getting ahead of myself. Oregon is a geographically large state, and this car trip takes seven hours from the Willamette Valley, sometimes in sunny, warm spring weather, often through icy rain and even snow. I don't revisit many locations year after year because there are an incredible number of beautiful places and I have limited time on this planet. The exception—Malheur—calls me back again and again. This annual going-back-to-a-place allows for an intimacy and deep knowledge, a place-based knowing that cannot happen without time spent watching and listening.

After crossing the Cascade Mountains and descending into the dry sage lands of Eastern Oregon, my heart rate begins to slow. I start to observe what's around me instead of thinking about the farm chores on my never-ending to-do list. With the windows rolled down, I listen more intently. Hearing the far-off *karoo karoo* of sandhill cranes lures me in deeper. By the time we've been driving five hours, we're ready to rest for the night. We always stay at a funky motel in Burns the first night.

The next morning, we start birding in earnest. We drive slowly through Burns Pauite Reservation land, looking for songbirds and sandhill cranes. The quiet is absolute. In drought years when the refuge lacks adequate water, we often find more birds here. Black-headed grosbeaks and the brilliant orange of Bullock's orioles flash through the willows.

We drive along River Road and look for great horned owls in the massive cottonwood trees, the remnant of some old homestead. The good people of Harney County remain patient with visitors who walk through their neighborhoods peering through binoculars. We often spot yellow-rumped warblers feeding in the tops of lilac trees. Yellow warblers (identified by reddish streaks on the male's chest) might be starting to nest in the willows along the river.

When we've exhausted our annual haunts outside of Burns, we head slowly toward Frenchglen, population nine. We have a room reserved at Drovers' Inn, just behind the Frenchglen Hotel. Even though it's only fifty-nine miles south of Burns, with so much to absorb along the way it takes us all day to get there.

When we reach refuge headquarters, still about thirty miles from Frenchglen, we check the list that volunteers have posted where birders record unusual sightings. Perhaps someone saw a rose-breasted grosbeak or a black-and-white warbler. Refuge headquarters is a "hot spot" for migrating birds. The isolated concentration of water, protective trees, and feeding grounds is a lifeline along the migratory flyway. Hungry, exhausted birds flying overhead spot the water and think literally, a refuge. I am safe, I can land.

We spend the afternoon wandering the grounds: people-watching and bird-watching at its best. Photographers with two-foot-long zoom lenses gather on the deck; Swarovski spotting scopes and Zeiss binoculars abound. I love viewing cedar waxwings, with their black eyeliner markings, feeding in the voluptuous pink blossoms of the hawthorn tree. American white pelicans funnel high overhead, white dots against the periwinkle sky.

Orange and yellow western tanagers perch in the trees like Christmas ornaments. A black-billed magpie sits on her nest, her feathers gleaming iridescent in blue, black, and white. Background calls of *chi-ca-go* let us know California quail are nearby. We enjoy a visual and aural overload.

By 5 p.m., we meet up with our friends on the porch of

Drovers' Inn. Our group has taken all the rooms there and filled up half the Frenchglen Hotel as well. The oft-asked question, "whadya see?" can be heard. Part of the ritual includes sharing stories of the day. In one day the total bird count can amount to 75 species, with weekend totals of anywhere from 120 to 140. Cliff swallows nest in the eaves above our heads, swooping in and out of their mud nests to feed their young, oblivious to our chatter. Then we make our way across the lawn to the hotel where we enjoy dinner served family-style.

We almost fill the long tables in the dining room, but we can always squeeze in a camper or two who wants a hot meal in a dry, cozy space. After the high-carbohydrate dinner, we walk to the old homestead, accompanied by the constant whinnying of Wilson's snipes.

The following morning our dawn foray might be to Page Springs Campground—on my Top Three list of most beautiful places to camp. When there is a dusting of snow on Steens Mountain during the night, the morning walk is a bracing affair. The Donner und Blitzen (Thunder and Lightning) River flows along the east side of the campground at the base of the rimrock, creating excellent habitat for California towhees, vireos, elusive soras, and Virginia rails, often with newly hatched chicks that look just like cotton balls on pipe-cleaner legs. When someone finds an unusual bird species, the scene can resemble the paparazzi crowd on Oscars night.

Another favorite morning walk is up the hill above the Frenchglen Hotel. Mountain sheep gambol along the rimrock, and we always search for the golden eagle's nest about halfway up the escarpment to look for nesting activity. If there's been a good amount of rain, the wildflowers provide an extravagant carpet. Sandhill cranes move with an elegant, languid wing stroke across our field of vision. We listen for chukars, rock wrens, and my favorite: the canyon wren that sings a descending series of liquid notes—somehow both mournful and magical. These early hikes help whet our appetites for some plate-size pancakes.

After a hearty breakfast we often drive along the Central Patrol Road on the refuge, stopping to view bobolinks with their creamy apricot neckband, yellow-breasted chats, or pinkish-bellied Lewis's woodpeckers. We'll pack a picnic lunch and eat at Benson Pond. If we're lucky, we'll see pairs of elegant, impossibly long-necked trumpeter swans with their young.

Or we might drive off the refuge to Fields instead. The two best things about Fields: the chocolate milkshakes at the cafe and the birds that frequent the oasis across the road from the cafe. In dry years, it may be the only water within one hundred miles and birds know it! In an area about the size of a basketball court, a thick tangle of willows and downed cottonwoods serves as temporary respite for weary, migrating warblers, flycatchers, and vireos. Great horned owls tend their chicks in the trees.

The expansiveness of Oregon's high desert and the stillness of this sage country entrances and deeply affects me. I feel like I'm wearing time suspenders. The pace of our weekend forces me to be present in the moment. There is nothing to do but look and listen. I walk slowly enough to find the well-camouflaged killdeer eggs in their nest of rocks and hear the sharp *tsuk* of the marsh wren in the cattails. By keeping my eyes wide open to catch movement at the periphery, I witness a long-eared owl's display flight. The male flaps its wings below its body, producing a clapping sound as it rockets and descends near the female.

I relish the ritual of spring in Malheur. I'm thankful that President Roosevelt had the foresight to protect Malheur in perpetuity. May this refuge remain protected so our children's grandchildren can continue to experience this special place years from now and grow to respect and love it as I do.

Birding the Andes

Fuertes's Parrot

A bumpy, impossibly steep hour-and-a-half drive in open-air jeeps leaves us covered in dust from clayish road silt. When the road flattens out and we finally park, I am relieved. We had planned this birding trip to Colombia to celebrate my retirement, but at this moment I question my choice to bird the Andes rather than recline with an umbrella drink in my hand. A chaise lounge on the Riviera calls to me.

Getting here from Oregon required three flights and multiple days of driving over mountain passes that made my palms sweat. Pepto-Bismol fills my roiling gut as we look out over the vertigo-inducing drop-offs. This trip is designed to see as many birds as we can, resulting in long days squinting into a spotting scope, dozing in the van to catch up on the short nights of sleep, and eating quickly with binoculars always at the ready. It means Velcro-ing myself to our birding guide, Fabrice, so I can more quickly find the bird when he sees it. As my sister would say, "Are we having fun yet?"

The other two couples on this private trip are much better birders than I am. They seem to have a much higher tolerance for ten-hour birding days. My birding life list is still in its infancy, and I have only been at this for ten years. They have all been birding since their college days.

Needless to say, I'm fairly intimidated.

While I'm supposed to be focused on the birds, my thoughts wander. We see shrines to the Virgin Mary everywhere. She stands guard in school playgrounds, she peeks out from concrete altars along the curving mountain passes, and she blesses the front yard of many houses. It occurs to me that I could be keeping a life list of Virgin Marys along with my life list of birds. Every time we pass a Mary, the jeep driver crosses himself and then kisses all five fingers. I nervously wonder if he prays for a safe journey; these jeep tracks are a little sketchy.

On this trip I will reach two thousand species on my life list of birds. The serious birders on this tour can boast of lists with more than thirty-five hundred species. I approach this sport as I do all others—as a dilettante, rather than building toward expertise. My friend Suzi says it sounds better to call myself a Renaissance woman. Maybe it's my fear of leading a lopsided life. As a farmer, philanthropist, birder, former CEO, gardener, and grandma, I have too many irons in the proverbial fire. If I spent more time studying their field marks before leaving on the trip, the birds would be easier to spot in the jungle vines.

Whenever he finds a new bird, Fabrice flashes his bright green laser into the trees and drills us: "Where ees my spot? Look one meter to the right of my spot!" Born in the Alsace region of France, his accented English requires some interpretation. "Zis brush finch is gone. Merde!" When I don't find the bird right away, I feel the same sense of anxiety as being closely followed by a foursome on the golf course who want to play through. The birds don't allow you to take your time. They fly, they drop, they move left, they retreat to the back of the tree trunk.

Three parallel mountain ranges form the Andes: the Western, Central, and Eastern Cordillera. Our twenty-two-day birding tour focuses on the Western and Central Cordillera. Besides French and English, Fabrice also speaks fluent Spanish, which simplifies our group's trip through Colombia. Our tour starts in Bogota, heads north to Medellin (yes, *that* Medellin, famous for its drug lords and I remind myself that I am paying for this privilege), then south to Bolumbolo and on to Jardin. We bird primarily in private reserves, sanctuaries, and national parks. Following Jardin, it's on to Manizales, then to Ibague and back to Bogota in a counter-clockwise fashion.

Mid-trip our birding expedition gets rerouted due to a bridge washout from a rainstorm. The rainy season has just started; it is raining hard almost every day, accompanied by thunder and lightning.

By now we have adjusted to the 5 a.m. wakeup schedule. But today, we rise at 4 a.m. to meet the two jeeps parked in front of the hotel. We must venture high into the Andes to find the recently rediscovered Fuertes's parrot, also called the indigo-winged parrot, and possibly the rarest resident bird in Colombia. I am fascinated by the idea of seeing this ghost species. Listed as critically endangered, it is endemic to Colombia and can be found, if one is lucky, only in the Central Cordillera. We head out for Finca Corte de Real. We pass hummingbird feeders filled with sugar water out in the middle of nowhere on the jeep road. The logistics of this boggle my mind. I ask Fabrice, "Who keeps these filled?"

His matter-of-fact response, "The military."

Me, incredulous, "Really?!"

"Yes." Fabrice explains that there is even a bird named after the former head of the military because he was so fond of birding, when he wasn't busy ordering people to be killed.

At that last part I realize he has been pulling my leg during the entire conversation. His infectious enthusiasm and side-splitting story-telling keep us all in good humor even at this early hour.

*** * * ***

Our trip started in the dripping, foggy dark at a private lodge and reserve operated by ProAves. It is named for the bird that can be found there—the chestnut-capped piha. The lodge consists of six rooms, a kitchen, and an outdoor tin-roofed dining area. They have left the lights on for us. Beetles the size of small kittens are attracted to the lights and fly around crashing into the walls and us.

In the morning we awake to a beautiful garden with ten hummingbird feeders, numbered and arranged in a semicircle around the dining area. Hummers cover the feeders, especially first thing in the morning. You can pivot on your chair and easily see them all. Already up and on task Fabrice calls out bird names over the loud buzzing, "western emerald at number three ... crowned woodnymph at number six ... black-throated mango, number two ... green-crowned brilliant on the backside of feeder five ..." All this before my morning caffeine. I swing my binoculars from station to station feeling almost dizzy. So many new birds. Although we have gathered to eat, breakfast is an afterthought.

A small dead tree in the garden serves as a feeding station for tanagers, guans, and barbets. The lodge guide places plantains on several branches, and the birds make quick work of the feast. I identify an Andean guan mom and dad and watch them feed their baby a plantain. Almost three feet tall, both the male and female are dark with a large red wattle hanging from their necks. The tree bows under their weight. The red-headed barbet dazzles with his cherry red head and breast. Blue-gray tanagers are numerous; a few scrub tanagers show up. I like this kind of birding: pacing at a dull roar, getting glimpses long enough to see the field marks, and learning a bit about each bird's behavior.

It's the start of a slow seduction. Birding from a chair! Ease the client in gently with easy-to-see birds. On subsequent days add long hikes and longer jeep rides on impassable trails. By day five or six the client is habituated to little sleep and high altitude, and the guide can move on to spend hours trying to find skulky birds in the tangle of jungle vines. In the tour's latter days, our long waits are punctuated with moments of sheer exhilaration when we spot difficult-to-find birds. Intermittent reward systems have proven to work most effectively with lab mice. It seems to work just as well with birders. In retrospect, after we're home, I realize how cleverly this tour has been mapped.

* * *

We are just outside Los Nevados National Natural Park at 10,500 feet in high temperate forest to find the Fuertes's parrot. On the range map, a dot signifies the only place in the world the Fuertes's parrot has been seen. That dot has become a tantalizing beacon to the bird nerd in me. I have always been a list maker: what to pack for vacation, what to get done before the party, a daily to-do list, a weekly to-do list for longer-term projects, a household improvement project list for the year. I love to check things off. We get to check off a lot of bird species on this trip. This satisfies me enormously.

We wait for the flyout in the metallic sheen of early morning. The parrots roost in nearby trees. Dressed in four layers, we stamp our feet while eating our tailgate breakfast at the back of the jeep: bananas, papaya, coffee, peanut butter, warm *arepas* (thick tortillas that are a staple at breakfast and lunch), and tasteless white cheese. Much of the rain forest has been cleared. Cattle country surrounds a thin patch of remnant forest. We stand expectantly, hoping against hope that we will glimpse the bird. We are jumpy and fooled by the raucous call of a small group of speckle-faced parrots. The low *kwaa-ar* of scaly-naped parrots flying high overhead initially deceives us until Fabrice identifies them. Parrot species are notoriously difficult to identify because the birds usually fly at high altitude. The defining characteristics of parrot species can take concentrated discernment: Is the wing stroke deep and deliberate or fast and fluttery? Is the call low or high? As Fabrice describes this while the birds fly quickly overhead, I am trying to keep up and understand, because I DO NOT WANT TO MISS THIS BIRD.

After standing around for an hour, Fabrice's manic stacotto splits the quiet, "Zees is za bird! Zees is za bird!" Binoculars jump up in unison. We get a flash of the iridescent blue wings as the parrot banks to land on a tree. A collective gasp emanates from six mouths simultaneously. Another flies out, then a small group of five follows. Binoculars swing, following the birds overhead as two more appear. We have hit the birding jackpot! We bird until 10 a.m., finishing the morning with Cheshire cat grins. Twenty-one Fuertes's parrots! A birding moment like no other. I feel like a pilgrim at Tinker Creek, discovering something new that has been here all along.

I try to sear this needle-in-the-haystack moment into my consciousness. Twelve-hour days birding hard-to-find species, motion sick from torturous jeep rides, no personal time, barely enough time to take a shower, wearing clothes that remain damp from the previous day's humidity and rain, operating at the edge of my birding knowledge and Spanish language skills, and deeply sleep deprived. As my friend's daughter would say with scorn in her voice, "That's such a First World problem." And one I feel so lucky to experience.

Two Lifers before Breakfast

We wake at 4:45 a.m. at the Montezuma Eco-Lodge, a

building converted into four rooms with plywood separating each space. No sound privacy and no window screens, which translates to sharing the space with moths, cockroaches, and some chomping insects I can't identify. We leave at 5:15 a.m. for a forty-five-minute jeep drive up a steep, rocky track ending in an antenna array guarded by the Colombia National Army.

Our target species for the morning include the native chestnut-bellied flowerpiercer and near-endemic dusky-headed brush-finch. At almost nine thousand feet, we climb out of the jeeps and are struck by the view across the valley of Mount Tatama—a slick, shining heave of granite.

Almost immediately our guide hears some squeaky singing at a tree on the edge of the track. It could be a flowerpiercer, one of ten *Diglossa* species that specialize in nectar eating. Everyone in our group listens hard, trying to pinpoint the source. Suddenly, a lone chestnut-bellied flowerpiercer pops up to the top of a flowering tree. His mahogany belly stands out brilliantly against the bronzy-green vines and leaves of olive, glossy emerald, and jade green that weave together.

We find the second bird quickly, in bird-chasing time. Not too far from the flowerpiercer, again following the vocalization of a dusky-headed brush-finch, we zero in on a patch of tangly growth and see the brush-finch perched in the vegetation where Fabrice's laser light dances—he is dark, olive, and not a "looker."

It's only 7 a.m. and we've already scored both of the target species for this high elevation. We celebrate with a hearty jeep tailgate breakfast. Even the best birder in our group admits he thought he'd be able to find more of the birds himself. Jungle birding is hard. Without Fabrice it would be slow going indeed.

For the remainder of the morning we walk down the steep track, birding our way back to the bridge crossing the Claro River to rendezvous with the jeeps. Halfway down we encounter a group of sweating, camouflaged young men marching up the road, toting machine guns. I curse myself for reading too much before the start of this trip about guerillas (or as Fabrice pronounces it in Spanish, "goo-rias"), the Shining Path, and the Revolutionary Armed Forces of Colombia. Just last night I commented to one of the women in our group about how the Shining Path would make a great name for an alcohol and drug recovery program. But this is real. Our two groups abruptly come to a stop. I must admit we look a tad bit suspect. We have a spotting scope and multiple pairs of binoculars, we all wear khaki clothes and rubber boots, and several of us are jotting notes. If I were in the military, I would question what the heck we were doing at the top of a mountain in the middle of the jungle.

I ask Fabrice to find out if they will allow me to take their picture. Maybe a questionable strategy to ease the tension that has suddenly overtaken our group. He goes one further and must be telling them that I want my picture taken *with* them. As they nod and smile and adjust their guns to look more fierce, Fabrice pushes me into the group. I focus on not making eye contact and not getting too close. I don't want one of their guns to go off accidently.

Fabrice makes the gesture to move closer together for the picture. We comply, camera shutters click, and now we are all friends. None of them looks old enough to shave. Many *muchas gracias* are said, and then they march up the remainder of the road to their barracks. The circles that have formed under my armpits are not a result of the humidity.

As we make our way down the road, we encounter the endemic gold-ringed tanager—yellow-and-black head and green body with blue wings. Absolutely stunning—it looks like my granddaughter chose its colors for her coloring book. I love the tanager family. They are big enough to find and often have brilliant color combinations. Next Fabrice gets a black-and-gold tanager in the spotting scope. I don't get a look at the bird before it flies away because I have hung back up the road, around a bend, to pee. Leaving the group is strongly discouraged, but a girl's bladder can only hold on for so long.

At one point in the oppressive heat, we stop to play the call of the yellow-bellied antpitta. Plump and almost tailless, they look like feather-covered eggs balanced on light-blue legs skinny as pipe cleaners. For such awkward-looking birds, they move fast. *The Field Guide to the Birds of Colombia* describes antpittas as shy and elusive, with a picture of a guy sitting on a couch, smoking a pipe. We know we're in for a long wait. While we all have our binoculars trained on a likely spot in the tangle close to the ground, one moves across the road to our right in great nervous hops, and my fellow birder catches it out of the corner of her eye. To make sure we don't miss the bird a second time, one of us looks up the road, one of us looks down the road, the rest of us peer into five layers of jungle, and we wait again. It calls and calls but never reappears. In the hellish humidity, I have shed my long-sleeved cover-up down to my short-sleeved T-shirt. We move further down the track.

Fabrice hears a yellow-headed manakin. The bird's call sounds like snapping fingers, but it's actually the wings snapping together. It means we are near a lek (an area where display and courtship behavior occurs), and the manakin is trying to attract females to come in and mate.

Before we veer onto a barely discernible path that gets us closer to the lek, I stop to hurriedly tuck my pants into my socks to ward off crawly, stingy things. Vines trip me and low-hanging branches fwap me in the face as I try to make my way silently behind Fabrice. Manakins are hard to find unless they are on a lek, spending much of their day elaborately displaying in the understory. They sing and dance as though in a Broadway production. We wait silently, trying to find the straw-colored bird with the muted yellow head. He is cagey and knows we are not female manakins, so he stops making his snapping sound. We wait even longer while sweat sheets down our faces and arms.

After Fabrice thinks we have spent enough time looking for the bird, which is usually a half hour after my patience level has drained to zero, we head back toward the track, hunched over to avoid the whipping brambles. When we emerge, I find tiny itching welts covering both my arms. I rub Benedryl gel on top of my maximum-strength-DEET-covered, sunscreen-swathed arms. The cocktail of preventive lotions has clearly offered no protection against the array of jungle plants that look innocent enough until you brush against them.

We have been walking downhill for five hours and my calf muscles want to give out. We spy the jeeps just ahead. Thank the jungle goddess! It makes me a believer in the shade of nail polish I have painted on for this trip—Keys to My Karma.

Fabrice has not been to Montezuma before, and he quickly becomes frustrated by what he considers slow birding conditions, hearing a bird every fifteen minutes or so. "Merde, zees es so slow." In prior days, multiple birds call at the same time, making it difficult to discern the various songs. From my perspective, I feel accomplished and end the day with twenty-three new birds on my life list. The birds have all been some version of skulky and yet we saw ninety-one species. Not bad for slow conditions.

In the evening when we come together for dinner, we review our checklists, which keep getting longer and more impressive: striped cuckoo, collared trogan, whooping motmot, crimson-rumped toucanet, rufous spinetail, scaly-throated foliage-gleaner, orange-breasted fruiteater, and hummingbirds too obscenely beautiful to imagine let alone name.

* * *

On our final morning in Montezuma, we hear an impressively loud crescendo of notes as we make our way down the same track. None of the six in our group can find the bird because we are expecting a large bird that matches the heft of its voice. Finally, our guide spots the ochre-breasted tanager on a low horizontal branch on a tree ahead. It is our first bird of the day and the caffeine has not yet kicked in. The scene is incongruous; the nine-inch drab bird is hanging head down, butt in the air. The gape of its beak almost looks like its jaw is unhinged. He is belting out an aria as if the future of his species depends on it. And it does. What he lacks in color, he makes up for in singing effort, with a voice that would make any self-respecting female ochre-breasted tanager swoon.

In Otun Quimbaya Reserve

We stay two nights at the reserve headquarters in Otun Quimbaya on the west slope of the Central Andes, about sixty-five hundred feet in elevation. Deep thunder fills our sleep and slashing rain wakes us each morning. On the first morning at the reserve we start out in heavy mist. Today we expect to see a red-ruffed fruitcrow with its brilliant crimson throat and chest, azure-headed motmots, Cauca guans, and parakeets.

One of my birding compatriots, binoculars focused on a ghostly presence where the road disappears almost entirely into milky fog, says, "Is that a cow?" Being the cow expert in the group, I follow her gaze and see a four-legged animal with a long snout and very un-cow-like head, like an anteater on steroids. Finally, an animal I can recognize. "It's a tapir!" The animal placidly eats leaves on a branch that has fallen across the road. Savoring this rare experience, we stand and watch the endemic mountain tapir for a good ten minutes while it finishes its breakfast and then moves deliberately and quietly into the jungle. We all get pictures to help us believe it actually happened.

Not twenty minutes later, I spot a furry brownish-gray animal with short legs and a very long tail slip into the jungle near where the tapir has been. It turns out to be a tayra, one of the largest members of the weasel family. We joke about our expertise at finding large, slow-moving animals since we can't seem to find the tiny, twitching birds.

As the morning progresses, it becomes increasingly clear that Sunday in Colombia is all about family and getting out of the city. We witness incredibly fit members of an octogenerian running club move by us on the road at a respectable clip, followed by seriously fast cyclists getting their miles in before church. Then a diesel-spewing bus that barely fits on the road lumbers by, filled to overflowing with kids, grandmas, dogs, and sweethearts. Soon the bus heaves by in the opposite direction, empty. Then we notice the bus riders hiking down the hill toward us in small groups. We dodge motorcyclists zooming by. It's wonderful to see so many people enjoying the outdoors and each other, making the long drive from town.

* * *

On Monday we bird close to the lodge. I eagerly anticipate seeing the torrent duck. Unlike most birds, the female of this species rivals the male in terms of color and field marks. The female has a rufous chest and face, with black-and-white striations running the length of her back. The male has a white chest with black streaks and a white face and neck. We walk across a bridge over the Otun River and spot the female first. She perches on a rock in the middle of the river torrent. I love when that happens—when the bird is just where it's supposed to be. Then the male appears, and they take off diving and swimming against the strong current. We get a good long look.

On the other side of the bridge from the torrent ducks, we spot four tiny torrent tyrannulets (seriously, who makes up these names?), a species that also frequents rushing water. Lined up on a branch overhanging the river, they act like flycatchers, sallying over the water, snatching insects mid-air.

After a deliciously short morning of birding, we climb into the van for a long drive to Pueblo Rico, where we switch to four-by-four trucks for the final two-hour climb to our next mountain destination.

I begin to fall in love with Colombia. The people graciously welcome us. Every single person we encounter makes eye contact and greets us. Quick to laugh at themselves and circumstances, they show infinite patience with my poor Spanish. There is a disregard for the clock that encourages real conversation. The kind of time that we obsess with at home ceases to exist.

Because I am always an observer and a participant, I can see the absurdity in this bird-chasing drama. I am a dabbler, not fully committed to the single-mindedness that a trip like this requires. As one of my favorite travelers, Anthony Bourdain, says, "Live your life, man. You should not miss a place like this." By day seventeen, I am ready to dine in the urban jungle of Bogota and leave the bird finding to others. This trip to Colombia validates my inclination to live life a mile wide and an inch deep—a valuable lesson that chaise lounges and umbrella drinks cannot touch.

Home: An Oasis and Endless To-Do List

Waiting at the airport for the final leg of your flight, you check the weather app to prepare for what might greet you at home after three weeks away—a desiccated garden or sodden piles of fall leaves. You learn it has rained hard for the first time in ninety days. You left in deep summer but now it is fall.

You put the key in the lock and turn the doorknob, unsure of what to expect as this is the first time you have employed this house sitter. You are happy to be home. In your own space. On your own schedule. The quiet of the farm is absolute.

You open the front door. There are drifts of dog hair in the corners of the kitchen, trailing out to the dining and laundry rooms.

You lug your bags upstairs and poke your head into the guest bedroom where the sitter has slept. The comforter is wrinkled and bunchy looking. You inspect it closely. She has crammed it into the washer then the dryer to try to remove a (red wine?) stain. She was not successful.

Geriatric Lucy-dog has peed on the kitchen rug, making it stick to the floor. Didn't the house sitter ever notice her shoes sticking to the floor tile?

You sigh deeply.

The dogs are alive.

The house did not burn down.

The raised beds in the garden look as though they were never watered. The garden desperately needs picking, even though you asked her to pick it often so the plants would continue to produce vegetables. The house sitter had a friend over to help her pick the garden once in the three weeks we were gone. We know this because the friend tore down our driveway so fast he kicked up gravel into our neighbor's pasture where expensive horses graze, prompting an irate phone call from our neighbor while we were building sand castles with our granddaughters on Bethany Beach, Delaware.

You observe that the lawn is a jungle. How did it grow with no rain?

The daily to-do list for our house sitter included bringing in the newspaper from our box at the end of the driveway. You canceled newspaper delivery starting the day after you left and resumed delivery the day you returned to prevent newspapers from piling up and looking like an invitation to a burglar. It meant she would need to bring in two papers. Both are still in the delivery box.

The welcoming bouquet you left for her on the counter is now dead spikes. The water in the vase has completely evaporated.

The birdfeeders are empty. Not a bird in sight. Have they gone so long without food that they've abandoned our avian oasis?

When you go to fill up the car, you observe that the odometer has an extra nine hundred miles on it. You said she could borrow it if she needed and left the key on the counter. But really? That's almost the distance to Los Angeles from Springfield, Oregon. Did she ever spend time at the house, with the dogs, watering the garden, picking the garden? You are so pissed off that you can't even bring yourself to call her. You realize this is immature. And you don't care.

You sigh deeply.

Home: An Oasis and Endless To-Do List

The dogs are alive.
The house did not burn down.

You flush the downstairs toilet and remember that it needs fixing. You go out to the shed and recall you left the fava beans unshucked because you ran out of time before leaving. Ugh. That's a four-hour task. The remaining vegetables must be picked and pickled—carrots, beets, parsnips. That's at least a six-hour task. The tarragon must be picked before the first frost and bottled in vinegar. A short two-hour job. You think about all the leaves that need to be raked. Three hours minimum.

You unpack while trying to maintain that vacation feeling. You get in the hot tub. You realize these are all trivial matters and you're glad to be home. With eyes fresh from vacation, you notice how much older the dogs look. They are twelve and fourteen. You vow not to leave again until they have been put to rest in the pasture doggie cemetery.

You sigh deeply.
The dogs are alive.
The house did not burn down.

Home: An oasis and endless to-do list.

The Mundane and the Miracle

I am at the esthetician's getting a facial that promises to plump up my collagen. I splurge for the extra eye treatment for fine lines. Who am I fooling? My lines are no longer fine. They could be described as crinkles.

I know exactly what I will look like when I'm seventy, eighty. I will look like my mother. Drooping eyelids, flat butt, protuberant stomach, thinning, wiry hair, hands with big veins, calves that are still good-looking. Thank goodness for that last piece, at least. People ask me if I'm a runner, a dancer? No, I came out of the womb with these muscular calves. Mom's muscular calves were the engine that carried me on her bicycle to elementary school every morning for kindergarten.

At the tail end of my fifty-eighth year I felt strong. I picked up forty-five-pound irrigation pipe in the pasture with a twenty-two-year-old farm helper and held my own. And I could get out of bed the next day! I was lifting kettle bells at a gym called, wonderfully, Strength Lab.

Yet by the middle of my fifty-ninth year I suddenly felt medically vulnerable. My defining characteristic had always been my energy. I slowly realized I was bereft of that hyperkinetic elan that had defined my days. I complained to the doctor that I felt tired all the time and my hip ached. She diagnosed osteoarthritis in my left hip, hypothyroidism, and osteoporosis. My right arm falls asleep at night if I sleep on my right side. If I lie on my left side, my hip aches and I can't get to sleep. I felt like I was drowning in the grief of getting frail. Realizing things could be much worse, I try and take this all in stride.

Before fifty-eight, all I took were vitamins. I foolishly prided myself on this fact. When asked at a doctor's appointment for a list of medications, I felt virtuous when I replied "none."

Time has a way of punching pride in the gut. Mom lived twenty-four years more after her sixtieth birthday. Is that what I wish for myself? At least that.

As I sit on the deck with a glass of wine and enjoy the waning days of my fifty-ninth year, the mundane that clutters my thoughts are:

Realizing that the farmhouse and vegetable garden will never both be clean and tidy at the same time; one must suffer for the other.

My carbon footprint.

Should I consider botox?

Am I taking enough risks?

Should we plant a hazelnut orchard on our farm as an act of faith or to hedge our bets?

Keeping track of my fourteen-year-old Lucy dog who has dementia and goes on walkabouts and can't recall how to get home.

Am I working out often enough?

Should I replace my fifteen-year-old-car?

Do I still have a modicum of sex appeal left?

Can we afford to schedule an international trip?

Should I finally learn to cook?

Wondering if I am a cool-enough grandma.

Am I contributing enough to the betterment of my community and planet?

Will my money run out before I do?

I know the answers will all work themselves out with time.

Based on the results of my most recent bone scan (compared with my baseline two years earlier) my primary care doctor prescribed Fosamax. It made me nervous as I had heard that it's bad for you to take this medication for more than five years, so what happens after year five? She said you take a year's vacation from the drug. Seven months later I had to have oral surgery because my upper back molar broke off and there wasn't enough bone left to adhere a crown. My endodontist said Fosamax is causing necrosis (death of bone tissue) and I should stop taking it. Confusing mixed messages. If I were relegated to taking this drug the rest of my life, I wanted to get it right.

I consulted with an endocrinologist. She recommended I do a blood panel and a twenty-four-hour urine test to see whether there were any underlying conditions accelerating the osteoporosis. Indeed, it turned out there were. The endocrinologist asked whether anyone in my family had ever had kidney stones. Yes, my dad. She asked further whether anyone in my family had ever had an autoimmune disease. Yes again, my dad. She asked whether I felt lethargic and fuzzy brained. I said yes, but I attributed that to menopause and getting older. All these yes answers, in combination with my test results, led her to a diagnosis of primary hyperparathyroidism.

When one or more of the parathyroid glands are overactive, our bones release calcium constantly into the blood stream. The result of too much parathyroid hormone is that bones lose their density and hardness. If that wasn't bad enough, the excess calcium removed from the bone stays in the blood, causing other problems. She recommended a parathyroidectomy; removing the parathyroid gland(s) would stop the rapid and continuous loss of bone density. She said, "You're young. You need to take care of this now." I loved her for that observation. Several recent studies have shown that the body can restore bone density after a parathyroidectomy. With that curative promise, I made an appointment to meet my surgeon.

Dr. Folek was young, with a capital Y. I must have been expressing some hesitation about being cut into. She assured me that the incision wouldn't show because she would line it up with one of the folds in my neck. I told her to watch her language. ... I do not have folds in my neck. (That is a lie.)

I scheduled surgery a week before leaving for my annual girlfriend trip, hoping for a smooth, speedy recovery. I realized I was spending too much time worrying about my physical body, and I might miss the wonder in the midst.

Fast forward to three weeks post-surgery. I was back to walking every day, taking my strength training class, and playing golf. At my post-op appointment, my endocrinologist said, "You look healthy. I wish I was as healthy as you." For that comment, I decided all over again that I loved her.

To celebrate my recovery, George and I leave for a trip to the Eastern shore. I am sitting in my beach chair reading Brian Doyle's *Children & Other Wild Animals*, where Brian exclaims that we cannot be reminded enough that we are blessed beyond measure to see and savor all that makes life amazing and astounding—that there is astonishment available in every moment. I still want to be changed, moved, brought to tears, made to laugh out loud at the absurdity and beauty of life. I don't want my conversations to become organ recitals.

George has waded out chest deep into the surf and come upon a monarch, nearly drowned, barely alive, floating.

He brought the butterfly to me to rest on my beach towel and be shielded from the wind by the book I'm reading, which has now become a life-saving instrument. Whoever said reading doesn't save lives? Thank you Brian Doyle. George creates a cup of sorts from the towel, allowing the monarch's wings to dry in the sun. We watch its proboscis uncurling, touching the towel, trying to place itself in this new environment. Focused on living. Contemplating the fragility of life, we sit still in silent vigil, long enough that the monarch regathers itself and flies off into the nearby meadow. George and I share a teary high-five.

Celebrating Sixty in Bozeman

I spent a week in Bozeman, Montana, with my girlfriends from high school celebrating our respective sixtieth birthdays. Best friends for forty-two years. Girls my mom knew and I knew their moms.

Since graduating from high school in 1976, six of us have made an annual pilgrimage to a mutually agreed-upon rendezvous. Usually the beach but sometimes the mountains. This year's get-together was different. Mary's husband died suddenly and unexpectedly a month before the trip. She wasn't sure if she wanted to come. Eileen cares for her veteran brother who is struggling with an undiagnosed medical issue. She decided three weeks before our trip that she couldn't leave him alone for an entire week. I had a parathyroidectomy a week before the trip and was feeling fragile. The doctor had told me to watch for numbness in my hands. It would mean I wasn't yet getting enough calcium into my system. Maybe only four of us would join together this year. It wouldn't be our normal separation from the reality of our lives.

Barb rented the car—an Armada—so big it deserved its own zip code. Teri arranged for the VRBO house in a neighborhood near downtown Bozeman. Michele was in charge of the book discussion for our once-a-year book group. Mary decided to join in after all. She was present physically, but lost spiritually.

It fell to me to organize activities. Usually our times together were crammed into a long weekend of talking late into the night, fueled by chips, guacamole, and margaritas. In honor of our collective sixtieth, we had scheduled an entire week together. That would require several organized outings, or we might end up driving each other crazy.

Monday was a half-day paddle raft trip on the Yellowstone River. It was a gorgeous seventy-five-degree morning in mid-July. We wore bathing suit tops and shorts. By the time we reached Gardiner, blue sky had turned metallic and intermittent rain spit down. Our guide was twenty-two-year-old Karch. As we listened to his safety talk, the rain became more insistent. Barb and I had volunteered for front paddler positions, the wettest seats in the inflatable. Halfway through the eight-river-mile trip, thunder boomed over the nearby mountains. My hands started to go numb. I was having a hard time holding onto the paddle. It was a cold, two-and-a-half-hour paddle through Class II rapids. Exhausted and wet, I gobbled down calcium pills back at the car.

After dinner that evening we hiked up Peet's Hill to watch the sun set. A pinkening sky slowly radiated outward as the sun dropped behind the Gallatin Range. We sat on the front porch that night and every night that week with glasses of wine and talked about whatever was on our minds. How lucky we felt to be together again. Our kids. Our grandkids. Retirement. The relentless pace of work (for those not retired). Traveling. Thoughts on turning sixty. How things can turn on a dime. With the delivery of a diagnosis. With the sudden, inexplicable death of a healthy husband. With a daughter who moved across the country and shut her mom out of her life entirely.

On Tuesday we roamed around downtown shops and found a dress for Mary to wear to the memorial service for Paul. She stayed at the house to write the eulogy, as the service was scheduled just five days after we all returned home.

Celebrating Sixty in Bozeman

Since Mary's Paul died, I'd been haunted by the fact that I could lose my husband in the blink of an eye—just like Mary. The entire week I avoided being alone with Mary, as if she were charged with some contagious, combustible force. I didn't want to catch it. Intellectually, I realized that the death of her husband wasn't contagious, but emotionally I was unprepared to inhabit that space. I struggled through our time together, even as Mary struggled with her newfound status of widower, dealing with her own and her stepkids' emotional states. I didn't know how to console her. I could not voice any of this. I hoped it was not apparent. I promised myself to do better when we met again—to be a better friend.

We perused the magazine section at Barnes & Noble for *MarysJanesFarm* because one of my essays was included in the latest issue. I read it out loud that evening to an appreciative audience. Old friends are so kind.

As we made dinner that night, Teri turned on hits from the 1970s and we listened to the soundtrack of our high school years, singing loudly to the Hall and Oates classic "Sara Smile," Carole King's "Tapestry," "Sweet-Talking Lover" by ELO, Carly Simon's "You're So Vain," and John Denver's "Rocky Mountain High." We got silly and start reciting each other's home addresses and land line numbers by heart. We all came from incredibly stable households with no divorced parents among us. None of us moved from our childhood homes until the day we left for college.

I don't have other friends that I break into song with. At sixty we've all become less neurotic, which lets us celebrate how much we have in common. We can join the group mood, confident that we're having a shared experience. Some years I felt exceptional, some just out of sync, always like I was orbiting outside the group, coming close at moments, but remaining apart from. Now it feels good to just be with these women who know me so well.

On Wednesday, we again drove from Bozeman to Gardiner, this time at 4 a.m. to meet up with a small van run by Yellowstone Forever that would take us into the Lamar Valley at the northeast end of the park to look for wildlife. Our viewing started earlier that morning in the pitch dark, however, when a herd of elk suddenly crossed the road in front of our car. Barb braked hard and avoided hitting any. Lots of shuddering deep breaths consumed the air in the car.

As the morning dawned and the fog lifted, we were lucky enough to see a mama black bear run across the road right in front of us, followed closely by her triplet cubs. Too cute for words. After navigating through cars backed up on either side of the road, the triplets immediately climbed into separate trees with mama anxiously patrolling the ground below.

We had an impromptu picnic along the Boiling River at the north entrance to the park.

On the drive back to Bozeman, we stopped at Grizzly Bear Encounter so some in the group could see a grizzly for the first time. It was a somewhat worn and dilapidated rescue operation for grizzlies that would not survive in the wild. It was good to see the bears playing in the water but left me feeling empty and sad like when I used to go to the zoo.

Michele wanted to do something cultural. We were hard-pressed to come up with a plan in a place that is revered for its outdoorsy-ness. Fly-fishing, yes. Horseback riding, check. River rafting, you bet. She spotted a craft night in the local paper and called to get details. A hysterical conversation ensued. Michele was talking glitter and glue. The person on the other end of the phone was talking IPAs and pilsners—craft night at the Ale Works.

Instead we ended up downtown at Bisl for an exquisite dinner.

On Friday morning we had a date with goats—a session

of goat yoga at Amaltheia Dairy Farm. We drove through the farm gate and were greeted by large goats in a pen who were quite curious about us as we got out of the car. I had lured everyone into this idea and was nervous that these goats were so big they would be too intimidating. Our yoga goddess, Abby, greeted us and indicated that we would be interacting with the younger, smaller goats in a secondary pen. Whew. She had mats spread out on the grass, with a trail of feed surrounding each mat to encourage the goats to interact with us as we did yoga poses. She admitted it was her first time leading a goat yoga class, and we all shared that it was our first time taking a goat yoga class. It was the goats' first time too. Growth mindset. We were all learners.

Abby had warned us to wear old clothes because the goats might pee and poop at random moments. I was in my element. Anything with animals! Teri was apprehensive. Barb was an engaged learner. Mary was at one with the goats, almost meditative. And Michele was game, as she is about most anything. After twenty minutes of actual yoga poses, Abby's gorgeous goat herder helper, Nick, led the goats back into their pen and we followed. The little bleaters were more interested in nibbling our clothes and nudging our thighs, wanting to be petted.

Even though these trips are far between, they are increasingly meaningful in the thread of continuity in my life. We mark the years by this annual ritual.

Before we left town on that bright Saturday morning, we took a last walk together through the neighborhood. We were wistful about leaving Bozeman and leaving each other. My friends, who would be joined by Eileen, would see each other at Paul's memorial later that week. My kids and grandkids were arriving that same Friday in Oregon, forcing me to miss the gathering. I knew it would probably be another year until I would see these soulmates of mine.

Grandparent Camp

Alyssia takes careful aim then douses Grandpa George in the face with her bucket of water. He shrieks. Evlyne laughs so hard she loses her balance and plops down into the wading pool, bottom first. An epic water fight ensues, much to our granddaughters' delight.

Our son and daughter-in-law, Nat and Ariana, are traveling on business and asked us to take care of our two granddaughters, seven-year-old Alyssia and three-year-old Evlyne, for a week. It's near the end of summer and the parents have exhausted all summer camp options—art camp, nature camp, music camp—and are now in need of Grandparent Camp to carry them over the hump until school starts in early September.

My husband and I are happy to oblige.

We fly from Oregon to Silver Spring, Maryland and arrive just in time for dinner on Sunday night. We eat on the patio and talk with the girls about the upcoming week. Ahead of our visit, we shipped art supplies, rocks (for painting), giant bubble wands, and ingredients to make slime.

Both parents leave early the next morning for work and a conference, and by the time they return, we will have navigated multiple melt-downs, sly requests for special treats, petitions to stay up past normal bedtime, poopy underwear, a peeing accident, appeals for double dessert for good behavior, and one I thought particularly imaginative—a solicitation to buy a "vacation souvenir" doll during the week of Grandparent Camp.

Have a structure, but be willing to improvise

I wake the first morning with the brilliant idea of sketching out the week ahead to get a sense of how the girls want to spend their time. I take a large sheet of art paper and make a grid with the day of the week on the horizontal axis and time blocks on the vertical. Ideas come fast and breathlessly. "I want to have Grandma paint my toenails." "I want to go to play at the park." "Let's play restaurant." "Mega water fight against Grandpa in the pool." "Read with Grandma." "Make a pie with Grandpa."

The upcoming Saturday is already fully scheduled with a morning birthday party at a petting farm and the county fair in the afternoon. There is an evening swim lesson mid-week that the girls need to attend. The time blocks quickly fill in. Alyssia insists that we start each day with a block titled "breakfast," because she is a very logical child. Evlyne is more scattershot about her approach.

We spend the majority of Monday morning painting rocks that we will hide in the nearby park for other kids to find. Alyssia is deeply into painting likenesses of the *Frozen* Princesses Anna and Elsa. She moves swiftly through all shades of blue and icy white in the paint set that we mailed ahead. She paints Olaf the Snowman. I focus on painting garden veggies and try to find rocks that match the shape of each vegetable. I paint an eggplant, beans, a carrot, and a tomato. Grandpa George and Evlyne focus on dinosaurs, rainbows, and ladybugs.

We clean up the paint mess then walk about a mile to the Greek restaurant for lunch because kids eat free on Mondays. Silver Spring is walkable, with restaurants, two grocery stores, a park, and the branch library all within easy walking distance from the girls' house. It is at least ninety degrees and 149 percent humidity. We fill up on gyros and calamari and head home.

Make sure there is time for silliness

Silliness is Grandpa's forte; he takes the lead. While the girls and Grandpa change into their bathing suits, fill the wading pool, and find their water weapons, I find towels and set out snacks for the ravenous aftermath. The girls are all hysterical giggles as they gang up on Grandpa George for an epic water fight. There is much chortling as the girls pour cold water down Grandpa's chest and back. Two hours later I dry them off and they sit outside eating their snacks.

Prepare them for success

Reading is a critical skill in life. We spend lots of time over the week reading. They love to be read to, especially silly stories and stories about doggies. Following a simple spaghetti dinner the girls change into their jammies and brush their teeth (after some coaxing). They clatter back downstairs for another reading marathon. Our son and daughter-in-law do not allow any screen time in the house, a rule we lovingly respect.

Tuesday is another sizzling day. Following breakfast, we walk about a mile to the library to return some books that are due and spend time in the children's section so the girls can pick out more books to take home. The self-checkout system is so simple, yet I miss the chunk-chunk of the librarian's stamping machine that I recall from my childhood.

Allow time for the imagination

Grandpa and the girls make slime and have fun using food dye to color it violet and turquoise. The slime-making is followed by an impromptu concert by Alyssia.

She strums her toy guitar and makes up song after song about slime. My favorite is called "Slime Out." I wish I had transcribed the words as they came tumbling out of her mouth, but the gist was something about her mom giving her a time out and Alyssia responding by saying she was going to slime out, not time out. Another, called "Slime Line," was about looking behind her and seeing that she was leaving a slime line, such a fine line. She emceed between songs, saying that she would be appearing in concert the following week with her full band.

Next up: Beauty Parlor. Aylssia makes a construction paper sign that says "Beauty Parlor" and another that says "Open" (on the back she has printed "Closed"). Alyssia and Evlyne pick out the color they want their fingernails and toenails painted. Grandma obliges. While their digits dry, I tame their extremely fine hair into ponytails and use sparkly clips to keep their "hairdos" in place. Then we take pictures and the Beauty Parlor closes for the day.

Repetition and ritual

After each active day together, the girls are famished. I am ready for bed. But I gather my waning energy while George makes dinner and I read them story after story because it is such an important ritual. Repetition and ritual help us all sleep well.

Mix it up—outdoor and indoor activities

Can it possibly be any more sweltering on Wednesday? Still, we need to get outside and use up some house-bound energy. Nat has asked us to make sure Alyssia spends some time bike riding. We haul the bike out of the shed and walk to the park. Alyssia does not feel comfortable on her bike. She still has training wheels on. We cajole, we plead, we get sharp, we use guilt—all to no avail. After raising the training wheels so she has to hold the bike in balance, I run alongside her on the bike path, holding on to the back of her bicycle seat. She is whining and using the brakes every time she feels out of control, which is often. I am soaking with sweat by the time I admit that it's just not going to happen. We are all pretty unhappy.

We put her bike away, load the painted rocks into a bag, and hop in the car to drive to the farmers' market in a nearby neighborhood. Along with the farmers selling produce, there are taco vendors. We decide to eat lunch there. On the way home, we stop at the park and hide the rocks by the play equipment and benches. Then it's time to swing and slide.

Be consistent and responsible in delivering the girls to their scheduled activities

Back at home the girls change into their swimsuits for swimming lessons. The pool is a twenty-five-minute drive from their house. On the way there, Alyssia tells us that she doesn't like the way the instructor makes her put her arms over her head and join each hand up to the other as she strokes forward. She'd rather swim the way her mommy taught her. When we arrive, I gird myself for a battle to get her in the pool, but she is acquiescent and demonstrates to the instructor that she has mastered freestyle so she can move to the next level.

Evlyne joins the other three-year-olds in the pool with a different instructor. In Evlyne's class she is required to put her entire head under water. She just barely submerges her head long enough for it to pass muster. The next part of the lesson involves sitting on the side of the pool and launching herself into the instructor's arms. This she loves, sporting her infectious grin.

Afterward I take them into the shower and wash their hair and get them dried off and changed. We stop for dinner at an Italian restaurant on our way home.

Grandma's choice

On Thursday we take the girls to Sandy Hook Beach. Finally, escape from the heat! We invent games to play on the way there. Every time they see a truck they call out its size—"Big Truck." When they see a dump truck they call out "Dump Truck." When they tire of this we sing songs.

After navigating lots of freeway traffic, Grandpa is relieved to get there and have the noise level subside. We cart backpacks, beach chairs, a tote filled with towels, a picnic lunch, and sand castle-making buckets and shovels from the car to the swimming beach. We find a place in the shade to set up our chairs. After Evlyne is outfitted with water wings and Alyssia puts on a life jacket, the girls immediately run into the water, where they stay for two hours. I have one eye on my book—*The Lager Queen of Minnesota*—and one eye on the girls.

Then sand castle construction starts in earnest. Grandpa and I find feathers and pearly shells to adorn the ramparts. After our picnic of peanut-butter-and-jelly sandwiches and fruit, the girls head back into the water for another two hours of play.

Then I decide it's so hot we all need ice cream. We walk over to a snack bar, and Alyssia orders a blueberry smoothie and Evlyne has a strawberry snow cone. I order a vanilla soft cone. It melts so fast we just barely make it back in time to share it with Grandpa. The girls' tongues and lips are dyed blue and pink, which they think is delightful. We pile back into the car and head home to avoid afternoon commuter traffic. The girls both crash and sleep the entire trip home.

We arrive home and they are ready to play. Grandpa needs a nap. So the girls and I take the fat sidewalk chalk to the backyard and color the bricks of their house that are within reach, since they live in a neighborhood that has no sidewalks. I figured it must be a permitted game as other bricks have already been chalked.

Don't just watch them play; play with them

With Grandpa awake, it's time to mix up the bubble soap and use our big bubble wands. We have one bucket of soap to share, so each of us takes a turn dipping our wands into the bucket until this devolves with the girls taking cuts in line in front of Grandma. I keep saying "Excuse me!" in my best British accent, which they mimic when they cut in front of me. They think this is hysterical.

Grandpa makes tacos for dinner. We serve them with nectarine slices. They know there is apple pie for dessert because they helped Grandpa make it yesterday. Making apple pie with Grandpa is part of every visit.

Friday morning after a breakfast of cereal and peaches, we make butter. It's easy to do; it just requires a lot of arm shaking. You start with a bottle of pasteurized whipping cream and shake the contents until the whey starts to separate from the cream. To set the tone, Grandpa finds The Beatles singing "Twist and Shout" on his phone so Grandma can shake the cream while twirling around and doing the twist. The girls love to dance, and we all prance around the kitchen when it is our turn to shake the jar. We set the butter in the refrigerator and use it later to make chocolate chip cookies.

Leave room for spontaneity

Since the butter-making doesn't take long, the girls decide they have time to play "Restaurant" before we go to the park to ride scooters. Evlyne takes our food orders, and Alyssia whips up the make-believe meals on their play stove. Alyssia writes up our bill, and we pretend to pay but leave real coins for a tip. This small amount of money goes into their allowance jar. We move through many, many courses, and then Alyssia hangs up the Closed sign when I say it's time to go to the park.

Wear them out so they sleep well

We drag their scooters and helmets up from the basement, since there is no garage in which to store equipment. We walk behind the girls as they scooter to the park. On the park pathway they are fearless and fast. Evlyne tries to keep up with Alyssia and is soon puffing and chuffing away. I get my walk in; Grandpa sits on a bench. The swings and slides beckon. I lift Evlyne up to reach the monkey bars, but she can't hold on and drops to her feet. We repeat this several times, her with a wild grin on her face. She laughs easily, and her laugh is contagious. After almost an hour at the park, we scooter back home for lunch.

The girls fill up on dinner leftovers, yogurt, and fruit. Then it's time to make chocolate chip cookies. Alyssia helps me measure ingredients and Evlyne helps stir. They each get to dip a spoon into the batter, and I show them how to scrape the batter off the spoon with their finger to form a cookie. It takes a long time to fill two cookie sheets. I am the epitome of patience. They get to lick the beaters and then it's off to bed after brushing their teeth.

Schedule recuperative time

I realize that its easier to do this when there are two of you on grandparent duty. You can spell each other. One can take a nap while the other plays with the grandkids. Nat is due home tonight, and it's his company night out at the Nationals baseball stadium. I am not a baseball fan, so when Nat offers me a ticket, I demur. The plan is for Grandpa George to take the girls on the subway into D.C. and meet up with Nat on the platform where two lines cross. The girls are excited because it means hot dogs and ice cream and staying out past their bedtime. I'm nervous about Grandpa navigating the Metro with the girls in tow and actually finding Nat in the throng of commuters. If successful, the four of them will walk together to the field from the Metro stop.

The evening is my own. I am alone. How sweet the sound of that word. I am exhausted by being out of my normal routine. I walk to dinner ALL BY MYSELF. I stop and listen to a busker drumming on an overturned plastic bucket. I throw the wad of ones I have in my wallet into his hat. The evening stretches out before me. I bring my book to read while I eat and people watch.

Ariana arrives home late that night.

The family leaves early Saturday for a birthday party at a petting farm. Blissfully, George and I have time to go visit a couple who live in the D.C. area. We spend brunch with our friends and then wander into Prose and Politics Bookstore—one of my favorite pastimes. I easily lose track of time in bookstores. We hurry back home.

Put on your game face

At the county fair that afternoon it's sticky and muggy. We start by walking though the barns to see the cows and bunnies and chickens. The smell of manure permeates the stale air, and maybe we're beginning to smell as well. We sit in the shade to watch a beekeeper demonstrate how honey is made. Mom, Dad, and the girls go on several rides. We watch the pig races and eat tasteless barbecue. The girls drink a shared lemonade, which causes a meltdown over unequally consumed shares. The rides make me nauseous; the food is fried and fatty. I try my hand at one of the games designed to rob me of my money. Incredibly, I win two stuffed giraffes. By the time I present them to the girls, they are both in sugar comas and exhausted from Grandparent Camp.

We leave the next afternoon after one last reading marathon. It has been a great week. We are all ready to get back to our routines. George and I are glad this camp lasts no longer than a week, but we miss the energy and giggles. We hum the "Slime Out" song when we're sitting in the hot tub reviewing the week's memorable moments.

When we call Nat and Ariana the following week to see how Alyssia and Evlyne are doing with the start of school, they tell us that the girls said of all the camps they attended that summer, they loved Grandparent Camp the best!

Swimming Lessons

Watching our granddaughters at swim lessons during Grandparent Camp sent me down memory lane, but what a contrast. I could never really get the hang of diving and I hated the feeling of water getting in my ears. I felt relieved to see that their classes have been more fun for them than mine were for me.

It was ninety degrees and 149 percent humidity as Grandpa George and our two granddaughters piled into the hot car to drive twenty-five miles to the private Kids First Swim Center. The girls wore their one-piece swimsuits and goggles for their weekly swim lessons. I hefted a canvas tote bag filled with towels, dry clothes to change into, shampoo, and flip-flops. It was an indoor pool in a non-descript commercial shopping mall. Both girls had to complete two more items on the list in order to pass to the next level. Evlyne, three, had to fully dunk her head underwater for a short count and Alyssia, seven, had to swim the width of the pool, freestyle.

Earlier that week when we took the girls to the seashore, Alyssia informed me that she doesn't like swimming freestyle because she has to bring her pointed hands together with her arms outstretched in front of her head to finish each stroke. She prefers the breast stroke. Then she demonstrated her version of a starfish, face down in the ocean, legs and arms akimbo. Evlyne, not to be outdone by her older sister, demonstrated her version of a freestyle stroke, hands together as though in prayer, arms raised over her head, covering her ears. Evlyne is game. As long as her sister is willing to get in the water, she is too. I pointed out the obvious. Swimming is a skill they can use their entire lives. Alyssia said, "You sound just like Mommy."

As we entered the building, the strong smell of chlorine assaulted my nostrils and transported me back to the summer when I was seven and took swimming lessons: water in my ears, chlorine up my nose, and green hair from too much pool time. In an effort to be upbeat, I asked Evlyne what's the best part about swimming lessons. She answered that it was when the instructor threw plastic ducks into the water and she had to swim after them and take them back to the side of the pool. Their swimming instructors use a kind and fun approach, emphasizing when something is done well.

I don't recall having a favorite part of swimming lessons. The pool seemed huge, the distance to swim a lap, long. The outdoor pool was surrounded by a concrete patio where parents could sit while their kids completed their lessons. Mom was determined that my sister and I learn to swim because she never had and she was uncomfortable around the water, would never even dip in her toe. She read her murder mystery while my sister and I were left to the mercy of the swim instructor.

My swim coach instructed us to dive in over his head while he stood in the pool at the edge. I remember feeling uncertain and out of my comfort zone. If we didn't swim with the proper stroke, he would pull us back to him by grabbing our ankles. This meant you got a nose full of chlorine water. How many times did this happen? All I remember is that I hated swim lessons.

The Kids First pool barely fit into the building. A narrow concrete path ran the length on one side, puddled with water, where parents could sit in plastic chairs and watch the lessons unfold through one-way windows that masquerade as mirrors on the pool side. With the low lighting, it felt a little claustrophobic and echoey, very different than learning at an open-air pool in the California sunshine.

Every summer my family would camp in the Sierra Nevadas. It was usually hot and my sister and I would keep cool by sitting in the creek. The year of the swimming lessons, after much whining, we were finally allowed to go to Mammoth Hot Springs to swim in the huge, Olympic-sized pool. I was a bit terrified by the enormous expanse of that pool. At the same time, the cool water lured me in.

Earlier that summer, I made up a game of traveling around the circumference of the bedroom I shared with my sister on the furniture and the beds. I would start balanced on the doorknob and swing the door with body momentum to get close enough to hop onto my bed, then onto my sister's desk, then her dresser, then her bed, then my dresser, then my desk, and then the vanity. Never touching the lime green shag carpeting. Pretty nifty. I attempted to repeat that in the pool. I was navigating around the edge of the pool holding on to the tile with my hands so my feet wouldn't touch the bottom of the pool. The lifeguard called me out, on his megaphone, no less. "Hey you in the purple bathing suit hanging onto the edge of the pool." Purple was my favorite color, so my ears perked up. Then I looked down at my bathing suit and looked up to him in his high lifeguard tower and realized maybe he was talking to me. I pointed to myself and he nodded. "I want to see you swim a lap or you'll have to get out of the deep end."

It's the first time I remember thinking, Don't underestimate me. I hated being called out for somehow under-performing. I'd be darned if I was going to accept that lifeguard's limited imagination about my ability to swim. I took a deep breath and pushed off hard from the side of the pool. I freestyled the length of that pool, kicking my stubby little legs to keep me afloat. Breathing hard and unsure I could make it, anger and humiliation fueled me.

I want my granddaughters to never be underestimated—to feel comfortable in the water as they get older, like they can take on any challenge and succeed. Isn't that every grandma's wish?

In the Vegetable Garden

A warm, early summer morning finds me in the garden watering and picking snow peas. An immature red-tailed hawk circling overhead punctuates the quiet, with its young voice a raspy imitation of its parents. It's not happy that mom and dad have forced it to fledge the nest and pitifully calls to them to be fed. From a nearby cottonwood tree, they keep one eye on junior with, I'm guessing, mounting frustration.

An Anna's hummingbird pokes its sharp bill into each periwinkle bachelor button blossom. Hummers love the orange and amber nasturtium tubes as well. Soon the hummingbird is joined by its mate, and they zoom straight up into the sky then over the roof of the house toward their nest hidden in the wisteria vine.

I plant my red plastic chair by a row of zinnias and gaze at the deep green potato plants with pink blossoms, knowing they will become Red La Soda potatoes by late July. A gentle breeze tickles the filigree of tiny leaves on the cilantro stalks. I don't have to visit the esthetician to get bee-stung lips from a shot of Restyline. I can get the same effect by sitting in the garden near the blossoming cilantro. Bees are attracted to the tiny blossoms and unbeknownst to me, one lands in my lemonade. I am, of course, busy reading, and grab my glass to take a sip and the bee stings me on the lower lip. And for that sun-kissed look, I don't need bronzers or self-tanning lotion. Spend-

In the Vegetable Garden

ing hours weeding and watering is a sure way to obtain a healthy glow.

Besides being a source of esthetician services, my garden is a place of serenity from which I gather my thoughts and inspiration. The weed-free loam between each row of onions and beans, snow peas and tomatoes fills me with pleasure. All I have to do is open the gate to the garden and I'm transported to a world of some truth I can't name. The tidiness lowers my blood pressure.

This garden restores my sense of purpose, my oneness with the earth. When the farm feels too overwhelming—prune a hundred walnut trees, cut sixty-six acres of pasture grass, repair three-hundred feet of barbed wire fence that the cows have loosened—this patch of land is my meditation on order. I water it and snow peas present themselves every morning to be harvested. I weed it, giving the herbs, vegetables, and flowers more room to grow. I take care of it and it takes care of me. It soothes my chaotic thoughts and allows me to forget about my never-ending chore list.

I lose track of time in the garden.

I construct a mental list of what will be ripe for picking when my granddaughters Alyssia and Evlyne arrive next week in late July. Potatoes, sunflowers, onions, basil, cauliflower, dill, carrots, beets, green beans, and broccoli will be ready to harvest.

Alyssia loves harvest time. When she and I walk out to the garden and pick what we're going to have with dinner, I tell her the dinner vegetable is her choice. Eating carrots just pulled from the soil is almost like eating candy, they are so sweet. We make silly mustaches with the green beans.

When Grandpa announces that it's time to dig the potatoes, Alyssia rushes to his side. Finding the treasures buried in the soil is like magic. We count how many each plant yields, so we can say we're practicing math. The buckets are too heavy for her to carry. In a few years she'll be able to do this by herself.

The black-capped chickadee chats noisily at me for getting too close to its nest as I water the celery row. I conjure up an idea to make the girls sashes they can wear diagonally across their chests, like my old Girl Scouts sash. I will find some stick-on badges that I'll award for hay-fort construction, helping in the garden, making s'mores over a fire pit in the backyard, and tent camping on the lawn.

Calendula are blooming right near the entrance gate, inviting the girls inside. I want to convey a love of nature to the girls.

Our neighbors had a fire in their well and can't get water to the cows, so we are babysitting the cows in our pasture. We have a gate that connects our properties. The cows feed in the corners where the hay mower can't reach, which is a benefit for us. Win-win. Midday the cows head en masse to the shady corner to lie under the maple tree. Earlier this morning when I walked down to get the newspaper, all six calves had gathered in the corral, as though on their first foray away from their respective moms.

When I go back out in the garden to pick broccoli for dinner. the herd moves again to the water trough to slake their late-afternoon thirst. If I stay out here long enough, I will witness the herd completing a circumnavigation of the forty-acre pasture. They are creatures of habit. The immature red-tailed hawk has been crying the entire day. Fed up, mom (or dad) lands in the field and kills a vole. The young hawk gratefully lands next to its parent and eats. The parent flies off.

In early August we pull 250 pounds of onions from the soil and let them dry before we store them in the walk-in cooler. Shallots, potatoes, acorn, and delicata squash join the potatoes. Peppers, eggplant, cucumbers, and celery fill the back porch refrigerator. We plan our weekly dinner menu based on what's popping in the garden at that time. There is a richness and satisfaction in the ritual of eating our meals from the vegetable garden every day. Our grocery list becomes smaller and smaller until by late summer it consists only of cheese, eggs, lemons, limes, and bananas. Everything else we need is ripe or has been picked and stored in the walk-in cooler for the winter. Full circle.

On a cold winter afternoon, we'll defrost a cut of black Angus from the steer we butchered in early fall and add in potatoes and onions from the cooler to make a hearty stew, flavored with lemongrass and Thai basil. It's gratifying to eat locally sourced (backyard) deliciousness. This is the place I want to be—living a homemade life in this digital world.

Out on a Limb

We buy oiled sunflower seed in fifty-pound bags at the local farm store. Our resident crew of feathered friends makes quick work of this bounty at our five feeders. As I scramble an egg, I can hear the *dee-dee-dee* of the chickadees fueling up in the brisk morning chill. If I'm lucky a white-breasted nuthatch will arrive, always alone, and quickly zoom in to get one seed at a time, flying back to the cover of the oak tree to crack open the seed.

As I sit down to breakfast, the scurrying troop of California quail moves into action in one large mass, pecking seed under the feeder in front of our dining room bay window. I have counted thirty-two feeding at a time. Ever cautious, they keep on the lookout for the sharp-shinned hawk that cleverly conceals himself in the nearby walnut tree. When I head out the kitchen door to get the newspaper, the quail scatter helter-skelter with a furious flapping of stubby wings. The lead quail *tsktsktsks* rapidly in alarm without taking a breath.

Pine siskins are sloppy eaters and leave plenty for the mourning doves. The doves like to congregate under the feeders, snatching up the seeds that fall to the ground.

House finches and American goldfinches prefer the feeder on the west side of the house, jockeying for position as we move deeper into the morning. My yard bird list has grown steadily in the last year after we installed ten new birdhouses on our garden fence posts. Combined with the cover that our vegetable garden provides and the food at our feeders, all that was missing was more housing.

Every year the killdeer pair nests in the same place—the rocky area between the garden and pasture. They usually arrive in late April or early May when we are planting rows of vegetable starts and seeds in our garden. The incubation period is short, about twenty-eight days. The male and female switch off nest duty. The male will fly within twenty feet of the nest, but never land right next to it. He will slowly circle in to take the female's place, while the female flies off to eat. It seems like they do this exchange every hour, but my statistical analysis is sorely lacking in data.

I slather bark butter on the wooden feeder for the scrub jays and Steller's jays. They can demolish four tablespoons of this high-fat diet in a half hour. I've never calculated how much I spend annually on bird feed because the delight I get from watching our feathered friends is incalculable. We co-exist in symbiosis; they receive food, I receive joy.

The other day as I was walking down the road that leads to our farm, a flash of periwinkle caught my eye. A ring-necked duck in breeding plumage with his gray-blue bill paddled alone in the creek, clearly looking for love. Further down the creek toward our house, I spotted the glossy emerald head and bright orange bill of a wood duck. I hope the two ducks weren't competing for territory.

The heavy winter rains ravaged our access road—a series of deep gouges needed filling. George estimated that two yards of gravel might be enough. On the first dry day, we loaded the pickup truck so full that its nose pointed to heaven and the tailgate sloped dangerously downward. I drove along our easement while my husband walked behind the truck shoveling gravel into the holes. With a pace of about three miles an hour, I had plenty of time to look around for birds. I spied the yellow-orange stiletto bill of a great egret poking down into the grassy shallows at creek's edge, spearing lunch.

When the Canada goose pair honks into view, circling in wide arcs, I crane my neck to witness a bombardier-like landing in the top of the cottonwood snag. One stations itself as lookout while the other lands smoothly on the water. They engage in a honking call and response as though reassuring each other.

Observing wild lives parallel to our own transforms the mundane into joyful surprises and shifts my sense of place, opening a portal into another realm. Caring for our yard birds is never a burden. It is a way to connect with them and, together, enjoy this place we all call home.

Pilates 1.0

I am a beginner. To stay limber and ease the arthritis in my hip, I take a leap and sign up for Pilates individual instruction at a private home. I go once a week. Each time I show up she asks me for a rundown of how my body's doing. It is early spring and our farm chore to-do list is at a seasonal high. Today my lower back is sore from picking up tree trimmings from a hundred walnut trees that grow along the border of our pasture. We had to clear the low-hanging branches to get the hay mower out to the edge of the pasture. She has me do some exercises that stretch my lower back.

The following week, the same query, "How's your body?"

"Yesterday I planted the last of the vegetable garden. Too many squats to count. My thighs are burning." My instructor notes this in her play book and we get to work on stretching my hip flexors.

That gets to the meat of the matter. Born with no hip socket on my left side, I didn't walk until I was three years old. During those three years, a cast covered the lower part of my body, starting at my rib cage and ending at my toes, splaying my legs at a 120-degree angle. Every so often the cast would be sawed off and the doctor would rotate my leg to a different angle, with the ultimate goal of forming a hip socket. It worked. My last leg braces were taken off in 1961. After that, I never stopped moving.

It has finally caught up with me. I suffer from hip impingement on my left side—there is just not enough space between the socket and the head of my femur to move my hip without pain.

Now it is early summer and it's time to cut hay, tedder the hay, windrow the hay, bale the hay, test the bales for moisture, load the bales onto a trailer, drive the trailer to the barn, and unload the bales. All this requires innumerable tromps across the myriad pastures when the equipment breaks down, when we run out of baling twine, when we run out of gas, when the mower needs oiling, when we run out of water in the ice chests, when one of our hay crew members has an allergic reaction and needs drugs administered.

"How's your body today?"

"My calves are cramping and my right arm falls asleep when I lie on that side in bed."

My instructor works her magic and keeps my synovial fluid lubricating my joints like a well-oiled baler. At the end of class she admonishes, "You should keep a self-care journal. You can't keep this pace up through the summer."

I burst out laughing. "It sounds pretty woo-woo. What does journaling self-care mean?"

"It keeps you intentional about taking care of your body. Your body works so hard for you."

"I sit in the hot tub every evening to soak my aching muscles, does that count? Does retail therapy count?" I roll my eyes. This isn't going to work for me.

She rolls her eyes. She shows me her self-care journal that includes how many hours of sleep she gets, how many glasses of water she drinks, her gluten intake, if she gets enough exercise (which seems pretty ridiculous to me since she is a PILATES INSTRUCTOR, for gawd's sake). I am taking Pilates, doesn't that count as self-care?

I share this story with members of my writing critique

group. I think they will agree that keeping a self-care journal is excessive and laugh along with me, but I am wrong. They all sit quietly while I look around the room for validation. One person volunteers that she keeps a journal of how often she meditates. Another says she tracks how many miles she walks each day to ensure that she limits her screen time and gets fresh air every afternoon. Who knew that everyone journaled their self-care except me? I am suspicious of this. What is the point?

I call my sister and moan, "I don't have time to journal my self-care!" She laughs and again I am suspicious, "Do you journal your self-care?" She responds with an emphatic "No!" Maybe this aversion to self-care is genetic? Stored somewhere deep in my DNA? More likely it comes from recalling my mother's mantra, "Why talk about it? Just take action." Or my maternal grandmother's admonition, "Idle hands are the devil's workshop."

Here's why I don't have time to journal my self-care. George and I and our hay crew must get the hay out of five fields before the rain starts. We must replant the broccoli that didn't come up and the pea seed that was eaten by the quail or we won't have any vegetables to eat. Buck up the trees that fell in the wind storm and get the wood split and stowed in the barn. Pressure wash and treat the decks to avoid dry rot. Paint the peeling trim and drip cap on the house. Put moss killer on the roofs of all the outbuildings and the house to ensure longevity. Clear out the weedy beds in the yard. Pick and can all the ripe tomatoes and make salsa, spaghetti sauce, diced tomatoes, and ketchup. Slice and dry apples from our two small trees. The list is ENDLESS.

In a moment of recognition at the absurdity of our never-ending chore list, realizing that I do need to take better care of myself, I make an appointment for a massage at a local spa. That is self-care, right? My husband says, "How long will that take? We have to put down gravel on the access road before the rain starts."

I live with a fifth-generation New England (read independent) farmer who refuses to hire anybody to do anything we can do ourselves. My notion that self-care is an unnecessary indulgence gets magnified ten-fold by my partner's ability to out-work me. How can I not keep up with him? He is twelve years older than I.

I abandon my Pilates instructor, not because of her admonishment to journal my self-care but because individual sessions are too expensive. George and I sign up for membership at our local parks department fitness center. I try out a Pilates class while George watches. He has had a tiny health scare, which has put the fear of God into him.

George, who thinks jeans are appropriate attire for any occasion—weddings, funerals, birding, bicycling, and holiday parties—will have to wear something different if he is to take Pilates.

The Pilates class is at 9 a.m., a bit early for this retired body to be up and limber. Each morning my arthritic hips and lower back require ten minutes of exercising in bed—including the hamstring nerve glide (where I lie on my back with both knees bent and cross one leg over the other, swinging my leg up and down from the knee), hip flexor stretches, and hip socket loosening—before my feet can hit the floor and my body is upright.

Once all this is completed, I shuffle to the bathroom to put on my yoga pants and toe socks. Maneuvering each individual toe into its proper compartment necessitates lots of scruntering. That would be defined as longwinded grunting, though not quite as guttural.

I am worn out by the time I've put both socks on! This does not bode well for sustaining an hour of core cardio, leg lifts, and remembering when to inhale and exhale. Nevertheless, I am ready to go.

We dig through the storage closet for a yoga mat

George assures me he has seen recently. It is in permanent curl position.

We drive to the fitness center. I find the class and battle to keep my mat unrolled as the instructor leads us in stretches. This mat issue is a bit of a distraction to my classmates, who have well-behaved mats. They also appear to have well-behaved balance. I teeter when we are instructed to balance on one tip-toed foot. Frankly, I teeter when asked to stand on both. I am not trying out for the ballet corps, so standing on my tiptoes seems unnecessary and perhaps should be covered in the Pilates 2.0 class.

We move on. The next position is called table top. We lie on our backs, raise our legs, bending at the knees so that our shins form a completely level table top, as though someone could set their cup of warm green tea on your shins without spilling a drop. And then hold that position while curling your head up to meet your knees, keeping your chin tucked. And up. And down. By this time my table top is tilting dangerously. Tea would be pooling on the floor near my butt. My faithful stomach muscles that helped me digest half a pizza last night have not shown up for class. They are still in a carbo coma from overindulgence.

Next we align our backs lengthwise along a foam roller, arms and legs outstretched to balance our bodies against the tendency to roll off the roller. The instructor says, "Don't forget to breathe." Sometimes I forget to breathe because I am busy making mental lists. She asks us to lift both legs in the air, bending at the knees and sway back and forth to stretch our lower backs. My roller has a mind of its own and wants to eject me. I counter with short, jerky movements to keep my balance. There is no grace and nothing easy about this. I channel Elizabeth Warren, thinking, Still, she persists. I manage through the class and feel pretty virtuous.

Once home, we order a mat for George and a thick pad for his knees just in case there are exercises that involve putting weight on your knees. He is covering all his bases. But he does not order sweatpants. I am internally shaking my head. He has searched his bookshelf and found a book about Pilates. He studies the exercises. This is how he approaches life. Study first, then commence. I am a dive-in-head-first kind of gal. Learn from doing. I honestly cannot recall why we have a Pilates book on the bookshelf. Did we try Pilates early in our marriage and I have blanked out the experience because it was awful?

The mat arrives by FedEx. George digs though a pile of clothes in our bedroom and finds a pair of sweatpants and we toddle off to class early the next morning. He is game and attempts all exercises, laugh-honking loudly when he can't quite get the rhythm of scissoring or core crunches.

I am proud of him. Just like my dad always told me, "You're never too old to learn something new."

Walking out of class, George says, "We're going to miss four Pilates classes while we're on our road trip."

"Hmmm?" I do the math and agree noncommittally.

"Do you think Julie (our instructor) would mind if we taped her? Then we could play the tape while we do the routine."

"You mean while we're on vacation?" I ask, incredulous. "Uh, we only have one roller."

"I can order another one online today so it gets here before we leave."

Who IS this man inhabiting my husband's body? I guess it shouldn't surprise me after thirty-two years of marriage. Single-minded focus is his approach to life. Pilates is now the focus. Now I'm tracking on the same wavelength.

"We can ask Julie if she's okay with us taping her."

Pilates 1.0

We sit on our mats on the beach in Southern California looking like any other Los Angelenos doing yoga on the beach with the notable absence of tanned, slim, sculpted physiques. None of the pictures you see of people peacefully doing yoga on the beach show sand whipping into their faces and curious seagulls hovering around looking for food. Nevertheless, we persist. Even though I have not once journaled my self-care, I'm feeling smug.

Actually, that is not what happens. We never unpack the mats and rollers from the car. There are too many cacti where we camp in the desert. There is too much wind where we camp at the beach. A hailstorm threatens one late afternoon. We get a room at a funky hotel and do not roll our mats onto the carpet. We do not mention Pilates. We exercise some self-care and find a bottle of wine buried in the ice chest, break out the Cheetos, and watch bad TV.

Autumnal Equinox Reset

I dread fall. The Autumnal Equinox is upon us and that means summer, my favorite season, is officially over. I equate fall with death because people close to me died in the fall. I put on my winter fat in the fall because I eat more. Then I feel bad about my lack of willpower. The days shorten. Sunsets become harder to find in the gray skies of October and November.

As I'm talking on the phone to a friend, I hear myself complaining and I decide that I need to change my mindset from a familiar groove of fall sadness to a growth mindset of fall gladness. We are in the seam that stitches summer to fall.

Starting with this day of the Autumnal Equinox, I decide to give myself the humble challenge of noticing One Beautiful Thing. Every. Day. And to respond joyfully.

Today, on my walk, I notice three deer lying in the sunshine on a grassy island in the creek. Seemingly content, they watch me as I walk by.

Yesterday, I waded into that very same creek to retrieve our plastic chairs that we sit in during the summer when the heat becomes too unbearable. Summer Creek Time, as we've dubbed it, is officially over. An iridescent green heron takes flight from its perch on a half-submerged log. They are not always easy to spot, so it feels auspicious somehow.

Today a man I encounter on my walk says, "I didn't

think it would be so hot." We are both wearing heavy polar fleece and sweating. I realize there is still warmth to celebrate with the beautiful sun on my paling skin.

At our weekly beer and blab gathering at a local restaurant, the owner unexpectedly stops by our table and says, "Thank you for being here every Thursday. The next round's on me."

At my Pilates class the following day, my instructor comments on my "guns" saying they look more sculpted. I have never appreciated my upper arms, yet her comment helps me recognize they are beautiful because they are strong.

When I open the bedroom curtains this morning, the ground fog lies thick on the pasture, making the cows shimmer in the distance.

Recent rains have greened up the pasture, turning the desiccated stubble into a lush blanket. The cows are happy.

The garden row of red, orange, and pink zinnias still blossom, voluptuous in the dimming light of this fall afternoon.

The honking call of Canada geese flying high overhead floats down to reach my ears as I cover the still-tender basil in the garden to ward off the frost predicted for tonight.

On my daily walk, I notice the burble of the creek has changed, becoming louder at a certain point deep in the shade. I peer closer with my binoculars and realize the gurgle is caused by a differential in creek height—a beaver has built a dam—not fifty feet from our house! I celebrate our new neighbor.

I enjoy the harvest-themed décor gracing the porches of many neighbors' homes. It makes me feel nostalgic for simpler times.

The next morning I head out to the garden to pick tarragon to make tarragon vinegar. It is absolutely still in the garden, but I hear the far-off rustle of the tall cottonwoods in our neighbor's field. The wind blows softly through the drying leaves. I wonder if the wind will soon reach my garden or if we don't have tall enough trees to "catch" the wind in our yard.

The dogwood leaves are turning deep burgundy, like a fine merlot.

This afternoon as I sweep off the kitchen porch, I notice a tiny green-and-brown frog sitting on one of the Halloween pumpkins near the drying corn stalks. Where did he come from? Is he sleeping? Is he injured? Is he trying to warm himself against the autumn chill?

I time my walk today in a dry window between rain showers. A fawn, with its fading spring spots, walks along the creek. Its mom must be nearby.

Tonight's sunset was spectacular. Tangerine sorbet, melding into the deep slate blue of an approaching front.

We head down to the Umpqua Valley to pick grapes before the first frost. We leave the house at 6:30 a.m. It is twenty-nine degrees and still dark outside. We barrel down Interstate 5 through thick fog. We meet Madelon, the owner, and Jeremy, the farm hand, at the vineyard and start picking pinot gris. The temperature has warmed to thirty-four degrees. Even though we wear layers of warm clothes, my hands soon feel wet and numb. The silent hush of the vineyard makes up for my frozen hands. By the time we are finished picking chardonnay grapes, the fog has started to burn off. We drive home in brilliant sunshine.

In the outdoor shed pressing grapes that afternoon, I hear a red-breasted nuthatch, one of my favorite birds because their call sounds like a child's toy horn. I associate them with forests and elevation, so I am pleased to hear the little chirper on our property.

I slather peanut butter on the feeder so the birds can build fat reserves to get them through the cold snap. It takes only ten minutes for the scrub jay to find the treat

Autumnal Equinox Reset

and start feeding. All his friends soon arrive. Happy hour at the bird feeder!

Tonight's harvest moon rises like a brilliant pumpkin. It seems a bit late in the game for this moon now. It is almost mid-October. But I'll take it!

After spreading moss killer on the roofs of the house and all the farm outbuildings, coating the deck to protect it for winter, and putting the scaffolding away from summer's house-painting job, my husband and I enjoy some much deserved bubbly in the hot tub. The pale apricot liquid effervesces delightfully in the stillness.

Walking through the park today, I come across an extremely shy pit bull walking beside her owner. The dog whimpers anxiously when I ask if I can pet her. Her owner explains that she has rescued her from a hoarding situation in Los Angeles and she is trying to socialize her. What sweet patience the owner demonstrates with her foster dog.

Driving to Philomath for a special lunch at Gathering Together Farm, we pass fields of purple cabbage and deep green kale that have not yet been picked. The tidy rows give me a sense of satisfaction. Corn mazes stand ready for Halloween tricksters and orange globes dot the fields.

Last night I dreamed that I registered #NoticeOneBeautifulThingEveryday and posted it on Instagram, something I don't even know how to do. It went viral. It became a movement. Somehow I was able to monetize it and became a millionaire. Aren't dreams strange?

This morning at sunrise, a red-tailed hawk sits in the cottonwood snag, silhouetted against a cotton-candy pink sky.

The waning gibbous moon shines through our bedroom window at 1:40 a.m. between downpours.

The crimson glory of the Japanese maple burns brightly in the front yard.

A great horned owl hoots quietly in a tree outside our

bedroom window at 4 a.m. It called for an hour but got no response.

When I tuck the fleece blanket around our German shorthaired pointer this chilly morning, he purrs contentedly. At thirteen years old, Bud spends most of his time curled on his bed.

By mid-day, the sun has broken through the heavy sky, lightening my mood.

We have friends over for a birthday drink and we all comment on the sunset—a cantaloupe-colored sky.

Sitting in the hot tub early this morning in the dense, wet fog, I can only hear, not see. The Canada geese migrate high overhead, a black-capped chickadee feeds near the garden, a far-off train whistle makes me want to travel.

Today we leave for Tasmania where it is sunny and spring. When we return there will be twenty-nine days until Winter Solstice.

When we arrive home, Bud's sweet grizzled face greets us at the kitchen door. Does he know we've been gone a month? I'm happy that he is still here with us on this planet.

The house sitter has raked into deep piles all the leaves that fell while we were gone. All we have to do is rake them onto tarps and pull the tarps out into the pasture in order to find our way through the yard to the bird feeders. What a relief to be spared doing this chore in the driving rain when the leaves are so heavy.

To kick off the holiday season, we attend a Friendsgiving feast with thirty wonderful, kind friends who I am thrilled to see and spend time with, feeling lucky that I am not lonely in this life.

My husband and I finish the final garden disassembly. The air is vibrant and crisp. The sun is out. We still have carrots, leeks, and beets in the ground that we can share with friends and eat for dinner on these cold, fall evenings.

I attend a book launch where a fellow writer reads from his newest book. It is so pure to see the love surrounding him from so many who are there to celebrate his achievement.

An acquaintance edited a manuscript for me while we were in Tasmania. When I meet with her she shares with me that she has a bit of a crush on me after having read my essays. She says, "They reveal so much about you, I feel like I have a new playmate." This is incredibly kind yet vulnerable of her to admit; I want to roll around on the ground like a puppy and revel in that feeling of total acceptance from a kindred spirit.

I receive a pre-Thanksgiving message from a dear friend thanking me for forty-three years of friendship. My heart is full.

It is dark and cold outside. Our forty-six-year-old heat pump has finally seized up in one last fit of effort. After many years of babying it along, it has to be replaced at a huge expense. Thankful to have heat from the fire burning in the fireplace, I sit on the couch with my legs outstretched, Bud lying between them on his bed. I am in the middle of a book that I can't put down. Life could be much worse.

Thanksgiving Day. We get a call from our younger son who is celebrating his wife's fifth anniversary of her bone marrow transplant. We are all thankful she is still alive. She finds meaning and hope in contributing to medical advances in managing chronic graft versus host disease by participating in a clinical trial of a new cancer drug.

A great blue heron hunkers over against the chill of Cedar Creek, looking for a fish breakfast.

The camellia is blooming! Its delicate, pearl-pink petals belie the fact that it is twenty degrees outside.

In today's mail George and I receive a homemade card from our seven-year-old granddaughter who has a strong command of vocabulary and spelling and loves exclamation points as much as I do. The message warms my heart. It reads, "For Grandma Cindy and Grandpa George. It is so much fun to be with you!! I love to pick vegetables with you in the garden!"

At 4 a.m. the coyote family sings to each other, yipping in delight. All join in—altos, sopranos, and tenors.

Finally Winter Solstice arrives. Waiting for the light to return, I have fashioned a way to navigate through the darkness. Soon the air will fill with the pungent aroma of blooming witch hazel. And the release of spring will follow with crocus, jonquils, and Lenten roses.

A Pig Named Noelle

Late morning on Christmas Eve day, things are quiet around the farm. Friends will arrive at 5 p.m. to share some bubbly and toast the holidays. A thousand-piece jigsaw puzzle depicting 1960s cereal boxes spreads across a table in the living room.

George has ordered delivery of three-quarter-minus gravel to repair the deep ruts in our access road. He hears the truck groaning down the driveway and goes out to meet the driver to show him where to dump the load.

The driver says, "Nice pig you have there."

George says, "What? We don't have a pig."

The driver says, "It scooted down your driveway in front of my truck and it's in your barn."

As I finish tidying the house for our guests, George texts me a picture of a bristly-looking creature lying on a bed of hay near our hay mower. I can't tell what it is.

I walk out to the barn to find out more about the situation. Sure enough, we have an odd-looking pig in our barn. Its coat is variegated cocoa brown and black with light gold bristles. We think it might be a pot-bellied pig, someone's pet that got loose. When I purse my lips and make kissing sounds, it comes toward me. I have no experience with pigs so I step backward, worried that it might charge me. Do pet pigs charge people? It is bigger than a mastiff—weighing maybe two hundred pounds. I try to get close enough to look into its eyes, and they don't look quite right. The eyelashes are bleached of color. It looks tired. Maybe it is blind? It trots back to the barn and crawls under the hay mower. Who knew pigs could crawl?

George and I decide it is sick and someone has dumped it on our driveway. We have absolutely no evidence to support this line of thinking, except our unfamiliarity with this type of pig. How else could it have come to be in our barn? Our barn is a long walk from any neighbors for such a short-legged creature.

People dump all sorts of things on our driveway. They think it's a dead-end street and therefore an appropriate place for rusted-out cars, deer carcasses, and feral cats. One time I caught a lady red-handed trying to "gift" us her pet goat she no longer wanted. She was driving around with the goat in her red hatchback Honda, looking for a place with lots of grass to dump it. I told her to keep her goat, thank you very much.

George looks on Craigslist to see if anyone is missing a pig or has a pig for sale. Coincidentally, someone in Marcola (across the McKenzie River and many miles from our farm) is offering a pig to a good home. We don't know what kind of pig, but I don't believe in coincidences.

I text a picture to my sister, and she quips, "What, no room at the inn for the baby?" I agree it might qualify as a Christmas miracle and name her Noelle.

George and I walk back to the house. He is recovering from a torn medial meniscus and needs to get off his feet. He Googles bristle-haired pig, and it turns out it is a Kune Kune breed. He calls Greenhill Humane Society to see if they will take the pig. They tell him that they don't deal with farm animals. He convinces them it is surely someone's lost pet.

George, continuing to be in charge of media and communication, texts our neighbor to see if she might know of any neighbors who keep pigs. She posts the pig's picture on the electronic neighborhood bulletin board and social media bulletin board. One of our neighbors owns two enormous pot-bellied pigs (each easily weighs six hundred pounds). There is conjecture that she might be missing one of her pigs. We quickly dispel that notion. Wrong size. Wrong color.

We are back to working on the jigsaw puzzle, resigning ourselves to someone's sick pig dying in our barn. I hear an odd squeal-like yelp, and say, "What was THAT?"

George, being a former pig farmer, says, "I know that sound." We hurry outside. Noelle is trying to get into the garden to eat the pumpkins she spotted. So much for the blind pig theory. She got zapped by the electric fence!

It is clear my afternoon is disappearing in pig details. I call my Pilates instructor to tell her I'm not going to make it to class because we are dealing with a lost pig. She says, "That is the lamest excuse I've ever heard. Text me a picture to prove it!"

I do. She texts me, "I'm posting it on Instagram!" Noelle will have her fifteen minutes of fame. Maybe someone will recognize her as their missing pig?

About this time, Greenhill calls us back to say they found a foster family who will take the pig and they'll be out with a van to pick her up in about an hour. So we have to get Noelle corralled.

George just happens to have some old rusted sheep panels stored in the barn from when he was a sheep farmer thirty-five years ago (and you know farmers never throw anything away). We set them up against the barn siding, forming a makeshift pigpen. I think to myself, "I could add pig corralling to my resume." George fills a wheelbarrow with three large pumpkins, wheels them over, and throws them into the pigpen so they splat open. Then we form a two-person nudging team behind Noelle to steer her toward the pen. We get her close, but she veers left behind the barn. George hobbles to the back side of the barn to cut her off. We are making progress on our second attempt until something spooks her and she runs back toward the garden. Who knew that pigs could run so fast? In my most cajoling voice I try to reassure Noelle. "Who's a good pig? Who's my best girl? I'm sorry you're lost honey. Aren't you hungry? Let's have some pumpkin."

She likes that idea. She is hungry. Maybe she has been on a long pig journey? We get her into the pen on the third try. She immediately snuffles into the pumpkin, snorting contentedly. She lets me pet her while she eats. Now that her strength is back, she tries to lift the sheep panels with her snout. I hold down the panels as George piles hay bales along the base so she won't be able to see out of the pen. We lay metal scaffolding across the top of the panels, and George parks the tractor with the bucket weighing down the metal scaffolding. I feel very thankful to have a former pig farmer at my side, developing ingenious solutions to each new issue that Noelle presents. The last thing we want is a pig loose on the farm with her steamrolling snout.

By this time it is getting dark. The shortest day of the year was only four days ago. Thankfully, the Greenhill van appears, followed by a second car with backup help. I motion the drivers to turn toward the barn. Two beautiful women saviors alight from their vehicles in designer jeans and boots that are not made for navigating pig poop. We discuss how we might get Noelle into the VERY LARGE dog crate that they've brought with them. They are appreciative that we've taken such good care of Noelle. We decide it's best to get the crate into the pen and put a pumpkin inside the crate to lure her in. Amazingly, our plan works!

Noelle fills the crate, snout to tail. We quickly remove all the hay bales and open the sheep panels. The two women and I lift the crate into the back of the van. George's knee is throbbing steadily and he is done for. He loads the rest of the pumpkins into the van so Noelle will have something to eat, because we're pretty sure that Greenhill doesn't stock pig food for foster pig families. We all stand close together in a group hug and say thank you for making this Christmas miracle have a happy ending. They drive away and we go inside to change our clothes so we don't smell like pig farmers when our friends arrive.

Post script: Three days later an article appears in the local newspaper stating that Susie the Pig has been reunited with her owner. It turns out that Susie escaped her pen from a farm about a mile and a half from our property. Maybe she got hungry? Maybe her owners were gone for the holidays and she got lonely? She traversed two neighbors' pastures, managing to avoid barbed wire fencing, circumnavigated a horse barn, and avoided a large herd of black Angus. She has quite a story to share with her grandpigs.

Cycles and Circles

The evening grosbeaks have returned to our feeders this gray November day. It is a celebration of the seasonal cycle. Like neon advertisements, they sport lime-green dayglow beaks and yellow-and-black plumage. They are not quiet, either. As they convene, they sound like they are starting up their engines with a whirring *reet, reet, reet.*

I am in the living room when I hear something slam against the kitchen window. All the evening grosbeaks are going crazy, calling in that hoarse metallic whir. I'm guessing the window has broken on impact. I look out the huge, still-intact double hung window and see a bird on the ground near our kitchen steps. It is on its back, doing a sickly imitation of a snow angel on the concrete, gasping for air. Should I go out and turn it over so it can right itself, or has it broken its neck with the impact against the window? I don't want to startle it and make matters worse, so I wait.

Five minutes later I hear a second slam against the glass and wonder if there is a mass suicide going on. On high alert, I look out the window and realize this second bird has suffered a significant loss of feathers and is sitting in shock on the gravel near the kitchen steps. What the heck is going on? Suddenly all is quiet at the feeder.

A Cooper's hawk or sharpie (sharp-shinned hawk) must have swooped in for an easy breakfast. Both these injured birds tried to escape and flew into the kitchen window, unable to gain enough height in their moment of stress to miss the house. I keep the dog inside, giving the two birds space to recover, if that's possible.

Just yesterday as I pulled into our driveway I noticed a large black Lab sitting placidly in our neighbors' front yard near the apple tree. Something struck me as odd about it and I backed up to get a better look. It was a huge beaver with a bright red apple in its mouth! I haven't seen one that size since the flood in 1996 when an exhausted beaver managed to eddy out of the creek rapids, his home destroyed by the floodwaters.

Farm life. I wouldn't have it any other way. But it does test my soul and my heart. Do we capture the raccoon in our garden that has been consuming our corn crop? Should the deer family of six get their fill of beans and sugar snap peas before we find a way to permanently chase them off from the garden? After all, life is a balance. We have displaced these animals by living here on the river.

But there's always work to be done to distract me from getting too caught up in the emotions that come with caring about animals. Before I moved to the farm, a stillbirth calf would have broken me in two. Being witness to heifers shot between the eyes on butchering day would have sent me to bed for days. I still sob. Living close to the land, not apart from it, has somehow inured me to this dance between life and death and inoculated me from being overwhelmed by sadness. There is grief and celebration both.

Cycles and circles.

I find myself apologizing to the covey of California quail we have living near our house. I go out to mow the lawn and they erupt in a flurry of wing, with their awkward low flight to the nearest cover. I hear the warning cry of the adult male when I get too close to the boxwoods. I say, "I'm just out here mowing the lawn. I have no ill intent."

Their daily pattern is to move from the cover of the rhododendrons to the cover of the boxwoods, then bullet across the yard to the feeder. They eat the sunflower seeds that have fallen under the feeder while the male sits on the top of the garden gate alert for any hawks overhead. At dusk, they move into the vegetable garden under cover of the dormant raspberry row. When we come out the back door to sit in the hot tub at night and let the dog out to pee before bedtime, the quail rush out from their cover and fly in their low frantic arc to roost in the cedar tree for the night.

We heard our first great horned owl of the season. Calling *Hoot. Hoot. Hoot.* Who? Who? Who? The male sounded like he was near the barn. The next morning we investigated and found remnants of two dead quail on the dirt floor of the barn.

Cycles and circles.

The grosbeak has miraculously managed to turn over onto her feet. She is sitting still, gathering herself. Fifteen minutes later she has flown into a nearby tree. The second bird is much worse off and I wonder if it has a concussion. Many of its tail feathers are missing, strewn about the steps leading to our kitchen door. George gently coaxes it into a nearby tree so it is protected from the hawk's eyes. Where has the hawk gone? Given up? I let out a deep breath. Wishing I could cure all things.

Celebration and grief, intertwined.

Grandma's Quilts

In this time of quarantining and longing for connection, I decided to check in the old-fashioned way and write a letter to my mom's best friend, Jackie. Mom passed fourteeen years ago, and other than sending an annual Christmas card, I hadn't been in touch with Jackie since then. I live in Oregon and she still lives in Los Angeles, where I grew up.

I had been thinking a lot about my friendships with girlfriends from high school and college and how important those relationships have been in my life. These friends have kept me sane on frequent Zoom calls, alleviating the isolation that comes with this pandemic lockdown. I felt compelled to tell Jackie how her friendship with my mom was a model for me. Their affection for each other demonstrated the importance and necessity of close friendships between women.

Jackie and Mom would sit out on the picnic table in the backyard, drink coffee, smoke cigarettes, and laugh at their most recent foibles or the latest Erma Bombeck column. Jackie has a surprising throwing-her-head-back laugh that is contagious. They were each other's mutual support group. Both my grandma, quilting in the living room, and I, doing homework in my bedroom, were privy to this joyous communion. I wanted that when I got old enough to have close women friends.

    Jackie surprised me with a phone call. The letter I sent had found her at a crossroads. She said she was packing up boxes for the moving company. She is eighty-seven and her daughter had finally convinced her to move across the country to live with her in Florida.

Before she enumerated how many boxes of fabric she was moving with her, she clarified, "I'm not a hoarder, I'm a collector." And laughed her infectious laugh. She and my mom shared a love of sewing and fabric collecting. She reminisced, "Everything your mom and I did together was fun and inexpensive." My conversation with Jackie never strayed too far from the topic of sewing. "Your mom taught me a lot about hand sewing," Jackie recalled. Mom and Jackie made Barbie clothes for four little girls—my sister and me and Jackie's two daughters.

After her husband, Carl, passed five years ago, Jackie explained that she spent her time making baby quilts for a local neonatal intensive care unit and dog beds for the Society for the Prevention of Cruelty to Animals. "I learned a lot from your grandmother, too," she said. "That's where I caught the quilting bug. Jeannette had no rotary blade, no rotary mat, no plastic grid to guide her, yet her corners were always perfect."

When I was growing up, my maternal grandmother lived with us. She was the consummate old-school quilter, hand-stitching beautiful quilts, twelve stitches to the inch, no piece larger than an inch and a half across. She made Grandmother's Flower Garden in hues of green for my sister and in multi-colored fabric for me. I also inherited two of her lovingly made quilts that are an intricate variation of the Eight-Pointed Star—one in red and white and one in purple and white. All her quilt tops were constructed with fabric scraps left from clothes Mom made for my sister and me. When I look at the quilts I can picture myself in those dresses. It's like a double treat. When Grandma died at age ninety-eight, she left Mom enough pieced quilt tops for three more full-size quilts. Mom never had the chance to finish those quilts. My older sister inherited them when Mom died. Sewing is a thread that connects three generations in my family.

When I turned sixty, my sister surprised me with a gift of one of those quilt tops, a Bear's Paw pattern made of wildly mismatched fabric that she had backed, bound, and quilted. It was a gift from my grandma and my mother, channeled through my sister.

As Jackie and I reached the end of our call, she said that she had something she wanted to send me that was precious to her and she wanted to make sure I'd be home to receive it. I couldn't fathom what it might be. A week later, a stunning Flower Basket quilt arrived in the mail—a gift Grandma had made for Jackie fifty-five years ago. Jackie wanted me to have it so it would be "back in the family."

Sunrise. Make Hay. Sunset.

I'm sitting out in the vegetable garden enjoying a freshly weeded, tidy view. George rides on the tractor, cutting hay in the west pasture. Our neighbor Dan tedders the cut hay in our north pasture. Turkey vultures circle overhead zeroing in on dead voles, mice, and moles—the unintended victims of the mower's blades.

It is mid-June, hot and dry. We share the annual labor and largesse of hay harvest with our neighbors Dan and Brenda. George cuts their pastures and ours. Dan puts the hay into windrows. Dan and Brenda both bale—we have two balers between our two families that allow us to make quick work of it when we get a favorable weather window of seven dry sunny days in a row. Some years in Western Oregon that's harder than you'd think. We want to cut the hay while it still has high nutritional value and not wait until the hot days in early July when it looks like straw. I coordinate the details. Line up the hay crew, organize dinners, make sure communication is timely between all parties, outfit the crew when they forget their hats and gloves, and orchestrate payday.

A coyote, with reddish ears and dappled coat of sable and black, hunted in the fields earlier this morning, pouncing on prey that attempted to hide in the windrows of cut hay. A curious crow cawed overhead, checking out the situation.

The hum of machinery is a soothing backdrop. My work in this annual ritual of haying will shift to high gear tomorrow, although we've been preparing for days, weeks. Repair broken mower blades; grease the mower, the rake, the balers. Drive to the farm supply store in the next county north of us to pick up parts. Replace the driveshaft on the mower. Clean out the barn of any remnant hay bales from last year. Move a stack of wood slated for construction of our tiny-house project. Line up a crew to load bales onto a trailer that I will pull, driving one of our neighbor's trucks.

Our crew is the local high school football team's offensive line. Serendipitously, the late afternoon when the weather pattern is right and we need the hay crew to start working, there is no football practice scheduled. My role is part mother—"Did you remember your gloves?" "Did you put allergy eye drops in?"—and part teacher—"Interweave the bales tightly so the stack won't collapse mid-winter and leave a mess in the barn."

They are young men who are still boys. For many this is their first paying job, and I need to instill behavior that is acceptable on a job site. Respect the boss. Support each other. No trash talk. Be reliable. Show up on time. If your trailer is finished first, go help the crew on the other trailer. We'll feed you well and reward you if you show up every day and work hard. We're counting on you. We have five fields to cut and we need you to commit to being here seven days in a row.

Back to my garden meditation. Finding a moment of peace before the wonderful chaos of harvesting a hundred tons of hay begins. For now, the mower is idled in the barn; cutting is finished for the day. We'll start baling tomorrow at 1:30 p.m. after the morning dew has dried. The crew will show up at 4 p.m., picking up bales and loading them into the barn until 8:30 p.m., and I will feed twelve hungry young men ten large pizzas. They will sit on the hay trailers and devour the pizza, watermelon slices, chocolate chip cookies, and water, water, water. And then it will all start over the following day.

As I ponder how to run a hay crew of sixteen-year-olds during this pandemic where social distancing is required by employers and the heat in the barn makes wearing a mask a claustrophobic endeavor, I am resigned to a state of hypervigilance—reminding them to pull their bandanas over their mouth and nose. We don't want our farm to be a COVID-19 hot spot, so we've queried them about their health, their travel over the last two weeks and ask for their cooperation in social distancing. They make all the right serious "Yes ma'am" responses and then move toward each other high-fiving and chest-bumping. I roll my eyes and remember what it was like to feel immortal. Exhale.

On the final day of haying two cars pull up near the barn. Owen and Grayson have shown up ten minutes early and I am impressed! They are both finishing fast-food hamburgers before they start work. I'm astounded at the amount of calories they consume and still stay so skinny. Was I ever able to eat like that?

The young men on our hay crew are unloading bales from the trailer and stacking them in the barn when suddenly a baby bird falls out of the nest that is tucked onto a roof truss above our heads. It lands on Owen's jean-clad thigh. In alarm, he says, "What do I do?" There is a wheelbarrow full of a split hay bale, and I quickly make a nest-like indentation in the middle. My husband says, "Hold still" to the startled young man and cups the baby in his gloved hand and gently nestles the chick into the wheelbarrow hay nest. "What kind is it?" Grayson asks. I tell them it's a black-capped chickadee, identifying its diminutive black cap half the size of a postage stamp. We all look up at the nest and wonder how the juvenile will be reunited with its mom. I feel sad that it might be unable to get back to the nest, back to its food source.

This all happens in an abbreviated moment. We go back to unloading bales. The next time I think to look at the wheelbarrow, the juvenile has disappeared. Now I'm worried it hopped out and someone will step on it or we'll run over it with the trailer. No time for worry. We have to get the remaining bales off the field before the rain starts. It is imminent.

Anne Lamott claims, "In order to be a writer, you have to learn to be reverent." And to "think of reverence as awe, as presence in and openness to the world." Again, as Lamott convincingly states, "writing motivates you to look closely at life." Farming presents us with these same opportunities. This ecstasy in paying attention is what keeps me tethered to the land. To be present in the field at spring migration when the birds wear their full breeding colors. To listen for the whistling, revving *chert* from the Bullock's oriole as she feeds in the red hot poker plant. To hear the mournful *karoo karoo* as the sandhill cranes fly languidly overhead. Inhale.

As we share socially distanced cocktails with neighbors in the barn to celebrate the end of a successful hay season, we get carried away with joy in watching the black phoebe build a nest in an adjacent oak tree. The crisp black-and-white fly-catching male arrived in our yard in mid-March at the start of the coronavirus quarantine. Every day he sat at the top of the birch tree or on a prominent perch on the pin oak and called and called, *tseee, tseee,* hoping to entice a mate to join him. I worried that he might never find a female, as this is only the second year he has nested in our yard. We see a female with him! Success! They are both speeding in and out of the barn, looking for nesting material. Celebration!

Gather

The next morning my husband spots the adult chickadee flying near the barn rafter with the juvenile fluttering near her. It found its own way back to the nest, not quite ready to fledge. Exhale.

Thank You

I am grateful to early readers who helped shape these essays: John Carter, Grace Elting Castle, John Daniel, Bronwyn Dean, Charleynne Gates, Laurie Gerloff, Keerti Hasija, Evelyn Searle Hess, Denise Jessup, Meg Kieran, Nancy Klobas, Jennifer Miley, Sallie Pappas, Kay Porter, Kirsten Steen, and Tom Titus. Sometimes I listened to your feedback and sometimes I didn't. I'm stubborn that way.

My idea of doing research involves shouting a question to my husband, who is on his computer in the next room, or calling my sister to verify facts about our growing-up years. Inevitably she remembers things I haven't and vice versa. Such is the nature of memory. Thank you to my stellar research team. All errors are mine alone.

Thank you to my family and cadre of dear friends who encourage and support me in my writing. You know who you are.

Deep appreciation to Suzi Prozanski and Kim Wollter for their editing prowess. Cartwheels of gratitude to Sherri Van Ravenhorst for her artistic sensibility.

I am grateful to Mom's best friend, Jackie Bauder, who generously shared anecdotes about my mom.

Posthumous thanks to Mom and Dad, who gave me the kind of childhood that is fun to write about because it's so full of sweet, innocent memories. My life is infinitely happier because they were optimists. I wish you could have met them. You'd love them too.

Most of all, a love letter to George. I am lucky enough to live with him on this farm. They both offer so much fodder for writing, in a good way.

A prayer of thanksgiving to Sun and Moon, Wind and Water, Earth and Sky. A standing ovation to this beautiful world. It inspires me every day.

"Sewing Frenzy" was first published in *Threads*, a publication of the Taunton Press in March 2018.

"Cooking Up Compassion" was first published as "Paella Alleviates Suffering in Community" in *Willamette Living* in November 2018.

"Out on a Limb" was first published in *MaryJanesFarm* in July 2019.

Cynthia Pappas lives with her husband and hound dog on a farm on the McKenzie River in Oregon. When she is not farming, she is binge reading or planning her next culinary travel adventure. Pappas is a retired Planned Parenthood CEO, birder, activist, gardener, and grandma. She is mom to two adult stepsons. She is the author of a memoir, *Homespun*. Gather is her second collection. Her essays have appeared in *Best Essays Northwest, Oregon Quarterly, The Eugene Register-Guard, Threads, MaryJanesFarm, Willamette Living, GreenPrints, Farm & Ranch Living,* and *Groundwaters.*

www.ingramcontent.com/pod-product-compliance
Lightning Source LLC
Chambersburg PA
CBHW071221090426
42736CB00014B/2929